market
kitchen
cookbook

market kitchen

cookbook featuring
recipes from rachel allen, matthew fort, amanda lamb, tom parker bowles, matt tebbutt and other great chefs.

Collins

HarperCollins*Publishers*
77–85 Fulham Palace Road,
Hammersmith, London W6 8JB

www.collins.co.uk

Collins® is a registered trademark of
HarperCollins*Publishers* Ltd

First published by Collins in 2010

10 9 8 7 6 5 4 3 2 1

goodfoodchannel.co.uk

Market Kitchen is broadcast daily on Good Food (Sky 249 and Virgin Media 260)

Text © Optomen Television 2010
Text design by Bob Vickers
Photographs © Philip Webb, except pages 12, 31, 33, 47, 84,169, 173 © Jean Cazals,
pages 6, 45, 59, 117, 137, 183 © Nicky Johnston.

Styling: Iris Bromet
Food styling: Joss Herd

optomen

Optomen Television asserts the moral right to be identified as the author of this work.

A catalogue record of this book is available from the British Library

ISBN 978-0-00-731459-1

Printed and bound in China by Leo Paper Products

contents

introduction

Welcome to the *Market Kitchen* cookbook, a collection of our favourite dishes from the popular TV programme hosted by a team of passionate food lovers: chef Matt Tebbutt, cook Rachel Allen, food writers Tom Parker Bowles and Matthew Fort, and home cook Amanda Lamb. They all love to cook, eat and talk about good food with Britain's best and well-known chefs, cooks and producers.

All our delicious food is cooked in a café studio kitchen and *Market Kitchen* takes its inspiration from the fresh, seasonal produce available at London's food mecca, Borough Market. Our recipes reflect what is available each day, from the first signs of spring with Jersey royal potatoes and asparagus, through the abundant strawberries and raspberries of June and July, to apples and pears in October.

In the colder months we celebrate imported seasonal treats such as blood oranges from Sicily and juicy alphonso mangoes from India. Our aim is to use the very best produce we can find from passionate producers and suppliers. Our producers' page at the back of the book allows you to share in our choice of the best sources of great ingredients.

Market Kitchen attracts the nation's finest chefs and cooks. Every week they serve up delicious dishes and you'll find many of them right here in our book. Raymond Blanc has re-created his Maman Blanc's recipe for vegetable soup, James Martin has reinvented the prawn cocktail, Richard Corrigan has rustled up a classic plate of fish, Gennaro Contaldo has revealed his favourite Bolognese recipe and Giorgio Locatelli has shown how he uses panettone in an Italian-style bread and butter pudding.

From our hob down at the Market you can find quick and simple suppers like Theo Randall's chocolate croccante, Jason Atherton's Vietnamese Pho, Tana Ramsay's Mackerel Niçoise, and fabulous recipes from the *Market Kitchen* presenting team. Try Matt Tebbutt's gastro pub classics and Rachel Allen's family food alongside Matthew Fort's generous helpings and Tom Parker Bowles' chilli delights. Amanda Lamb's favourite cheesecake recipe by her own brother is here too.

Alongside seasonality *Market Kitchen* champions simplicity and affordability. The recipes in this collection are easily achievable at home and often take only a few minutes to prepare. They taste good and usually don't break the bank, so do try them out on your family and friends.

The *Market Kitchen Cookbook* is bursting with great ideas for soups, salads, starters, all manner of vegetable and meat dishes, puddings and cakes, side dishes as well as a good collection of must-have storecupboard items. There is something for every day of the week, including delicious recipes for dinner parties and festive occasions. We hope this book will enable you to enjoy the mouthwatering flavours of the Market at home, whenever you want.

seasonal food at a glance

spring   **vegetables:** asparagus, basil, carrots, cauliflower, chervil, chicory, chives, dill, flat-leaf parsley, Jersey royal new potatoes, leeks, nettles, potatoes main crop, purple sprouting broccoli, radishes, rhubarb, rocket, sorrel, spinach, spring onions, watercress

         fruit: Alphonso mangos, bananas, lemons, passion fruit

summer   **vegetables:** artichoke, aubergine, basil, beetroot, broad beans, broccoli, carrots, chervil, chillies, chives, courgettes, cucumber, curly parsley, dill, fennel, flat-leaf parsley, French beans, garlic, kohlrabi, lettuce, mange tout, mint, nettles, new potatoes, onions, oregano, pak choi, peas, peppers, potatoes main crop, radishes, rhubarb, rocket, rosemary, runner beans, sage, sorrel, spinach, spring onions, sweetcorn, tarragon, thyme, turnips, watercress

         fruit: apricots, blackberries, blueberries, cherries, elderflowers, figs, gooseberries, greengages, kiwi fruit, loganberries, melons, nectarines, peaches, raspberries, redcurrants, strawberries, tomatoes

autumn   **vegetables:** artichoke, aubergine, basil, beetroot, broccoli, butternut squash, carrots, cavalo nero, celeriac, celery, chicory, chillies, chives, courgettes, cucumber, curly parsley, fennel, flat-leaf parsley, French beans, garlic, horseradish, Jerusalem artichoke, kale, kohlrabi, leeks, marrow, mint, onions, parsnips, peppers, potatoes main crop, pumpkin, radishes, rocket, rosemary, runner beans, sage, salsify, shallots, spinach, spring onions, swede, sweetcorn, tarragon, thyme, turnips, wild mushrooms

         fruit: almonds, Amalfi lemons, apples, blackberries, chestnuts, cobnuts, cranberries, damsons, figs, hazelnuts, medlars, melons, nectarines, passion fruit, peaches, pears, plums, quince, tomatoes, walnuts

winter   **vegetables:** beetroot, Brussels sprouts, carrots, cavalo nero, cauliflower, celeriac, celery, chicory, horseradish, Jerusalem artichoke, kale, leeks, onions, parsnips, potatoes main crop, rhubarb, salsify, shallots, spinach, swede, turnips

         fruit: almonds, Amalfi lemons, apples, bananas, blood oranges, chestnuts, clementines, cranberries, hazelnuts, kiwi fruit, lemons, oranges, passion fruit, pears, pineapple, pineapple, pomegranate, satsumas, tangerines, walnuts

soups, starters & salads

pappa al pomodoro

matt tebbutt

A great way to use up leftover ciabatta bread. Alongside basil, sage and Parmesan cheese, this recipe gives plain old tomato soup an Italian-style makeover.

serves 4

preparation time: 20 minutes
cooking time: 50 minutes

Olive oil, for frying
3 garlic cloves, peeled and cut
    into slivers
2 tsp chopped fresh sage
    leaves
6 ripe fresh plum tomatoes,
    peeled and chopped
400g (14oz) tin plum tomatoes
4 slices stale ciabatta bread,
    cut into chunks
Salt and freshly ground black
    pepper
800ml (1 1/2 pints) vegetable or
    chicken stock

to serve:
Fresh basil leaves, torn
Freshly grated Parmesan
    cheese
Extra virgin olive oil

In a large saucepan, heat a very generous layer of olive oil over a medium heat. Add the garlic followed by the sage and cook for 1–2 minutes until they give off a lovely smell and the garlic is golden.

Stir in the fresh tomatoes, then the tinned tomatoes and the bread. Stir well and season to taste, then pour in the stock and simmer for 45 minutes or until reduced. Taste for seasoning at the end. Serve at room temperature with the basil, Parmesan and plenty of extra virgin olive oil.

potato, chorizo and flat-leaf parsley soup

darina allen

Potatoes and onions form the base of most simple soups. If you don't have chorizo, red pepper purée or rocket pesto are good garnishes.

serves 4

preparation time: 15 minutes
cooking time: 30 minutes

40g (1¹/₂oz) butter
450g (1lb) potatoes, peeled and
    cut into 1cm (¹/₂in) dice
1 onion, peeled and cut into
    1cm (¹/₂in) dice
Salt and freshly ground black
    pepper
900ml (1¹/₂ pints) chicken or
    vegetable stock, preferably
    home-made
About 250ml (9fl oz) milk
12 slices chorizo
2 tbsp extra virgin olive oil
A large handful of fresh flat-leaf
    parsley, snipped

Melt the butter in a heavy-based saucepan. When it foams, add the potatoes and onion and toss in the butter until well coated. Sprinkle with 1 teaspoon of salt and a few grindings of pepper. Cover the vegetables closely with a butter wrapper or a disc of greaseproof paper and then the lid of the pan and sweat the vegetables over a gentle heat for about 10 minutes until softened.

Meanwhile, bring the stock to the boil in a separate pan. When the vegetables are tender but not coloured, add the hot stock and continue to cook for 15 minutes or until the vegetables are soft.

Purée the soup in a blender or food processor. Taste for seasoning and reheat, thinning it down with as much milk as you need for a good consistency.

Just before serving, fry the chorizo slices in the olive oil for 1–2 minutes on each side. Paprika-flavoured oil will render out of the chorizo.

To serve, float 3 chorizo slices on top of each bowl of soup, sprinkle with parsley and drizzle over a little chorizo oil.

cook's note
If the chorizo slices are large, cut them into bite-sized pieces before frying.

butter bean, chorizo and red onion soup

mark sargeant

Turn a tin of butterbeans from your store cupboard into a delicious warming soup for winter. Serve with fresh crusty bread.

serves 4

preparation time: 10 minutes
cooking time: 15 minutes

3 tbsp olive oil, plus extra for
    drizzling
225g (8oz) chorizo sausage,
    chopped into small bite-
    sized pieces
2 red onions, peeled and
    roughly diced
2 garlic cloves, peeled and very
    finely sliced
2 fresh thyme sprigs
Salt and freshly ground black
    pepper
2 x 420g tins butter beans,
    drained
1 small Savoy cabbage, outer
    leaves removed, cored and
    leaves roughly chopped
Grated zest of 1 lemon, plus
    squeeze of juice
A large handful of fresh parsley,
    roughly chopped
Crusty rolls, to serve

Heat the olive oil in a large heavy-based saucepan, add the chorizo and stir over a high heat for 2 minutes until the oil has taken on a reddish-brown hue from the chorizo. Add the onions, garlic and thyme and season lightly. Cook, stirring occasionally for 2–3 minutes.

Tip in the butter beans and stir so that all the ingredients are mixed and coated in the chorizo oil. Add enough boiling water to just cover them. Bring to a simmer and cook gently for about 2 minutes. Place the cabbage in the pan. Stir in a little water if necessary so there is enough liquid to cook the cabbage, then bring back to a simmer and cook for 5–7 minutes or until the cabbage is softened but still has a little crunch. When the cabbage is nearing the end of cooking, stir in the lemon zest and lemon juice. Scatter over the chopped parsley and cook for 30 seconds. Check the seasoning and adjust if necessary. Remove the thyme.

Ladle the soup into warm bowls and add a drizzle of olive oil and a grinding of pepper. Serve immediately with a crusty roll.

vietnamese pho

jason atherton

Pho is a Vietnamese soup, often eaten for breakfast. Try experimenting with other herbs and spices and different meat and vegetables.

serves 4

preparation time: 20 minutes
cooking time: 20 minutes

175g (6oz) fine dried rice noodles
A few handfuls of fresh mint
    leaves
A few handfuls of fresh coriander
    leaves, roughly chopped
1 fresh hot red chilli, deseeded
    and thinly sliced
6 large spring onions, trimmed
    and thinly sliced
1 lime, cut into wedges
Thai fish sauce
75g (3oz) fresh bean sprouts
275g (10oz) fillet steak, thinly
    sliced

for the broth:
1 beef stock cube
1 litre (1 3/4 pints) boiling water
900g (2lb) beef marrow bone
225g (8oz) piece shin of beef,
    chopped into large chunks
1 1/2 tsp black peppercorns
5 cloves
4 coriander seeds
1 cinnamon stick
3 star anise
5 green cardamom pods
3cm (1 1/4in) piece fresh root
    ginger, peeled and thickly
    sliced

Break the rice noodles into a large bowl, cover with lots of boiling water and leave to soak according to the packet instructions.

For the broth, crumble the stock cube into a large saucepan and pour in the boiling water. Add the marrow bone, the shin of beef and spices. Return to the boil, skim off any scum that rises to the surface, then reduce the heat and leave to simmer and take on the flavours while you prepare the rest of the ingredients.

Place the herbs, chilli, spring onions, lime wedges and some fish sauce into 5 separate small bowls so people can help themselves to each later. When the noodles are softened to the desired consistency, divide them and the bean sprouts among 4 large serving bowls.

Bring the broth back to a vigorous simmer. Take a large soup ladle and lay a quarter of the fillet steak slices over the sides of the ladle. Dip the ladle into the boiling stock so the meat is covered and leave for 5–10 seconds until the beef has changed colour to pale pink. Pour the stock from the ladle, along with the beef slices, into one of the bowls and top up with extra broth to cover the noodles. Repeat the cooking of the steak for each of the bowls. Serve immediately with the small bowls of herbs, chilli and spring onions on the side for scattering over and the bowls of lime and fish sauce for seasoning.

vegetable and chervil soup

raymond blanc

Chervil is overlooked in Britain but in France it is regarded as an essential herb. Its flavour can be spoiled by heat so it should be added towards the end of the cooking process. If you can't buy chervil, use parsley as a substitute.

serves 4

preparation time: 15 minutes
cooking time: 15 minutes

1 onion, peeled and finely chopped
1 garlic clove, peeled and finely chopped
1 large carrot, peeled and finely sliced
1 leek, outer leaves removed, cut across into 1cm (1/2in) slices
2 celery sticks, trimmed and finely sliced
1 tbsp unsalted butter
1 tsp salt
A pinch of freshly ground white pepper
1 litre (1 3/4 pints) boiling water
1 large courgette, cut in half lengthways and cut across into 5mm (1/4in) slices
3 ripe tomatoes, quartered and roughly chopped

to serve:
1 tbsp unsalted butter or soured cream
A large handful of fresh chervil, finely chopped

In a large saucepan, sweat the onion, garlic, carrot, leek and celery in the butter over a medium heat for 5 minutes to extract maximum flavour without colouring. Season with the salt and pepper.

Add the boiling water, courgette and tomatoes (the boiling water will reduce the cooking time and also keep the colours lively) and fast boil for 5 minutes.

To serve, whisk in the butter or soured cream (or both) and add the chervil. Taste and correct the seasoning if required.

cook's note
The key to this soup is its fresh, clean flavour. It is critical that you do not muddy the wonderful flavours of your vegetables by over cooking. Just a few minutes will do.

caldo verde

the hairy bikers, dave myers and si king

This hearty soup is often claimed to be the national dish of Portugal. The perfect accompaniment is country-style bread.

serves 4 generously

preparation time: 20 minutes
cooking time: 35 minutes

5 tbsp olive oil
1 large onion, peeled and finely chopped
3 garlic cloves, peeled and crushed
200g (7oz) chorizo sausage, cut into chunks
4 large floury potatoes, peeled and diced
1 litre (1³/4 pints) vegetable or chicken stock
2 bay leaves
Salt and freshly ground black pepper
500g (1lb 2oz) leafy green vegetables, such as cabbage, finely sliced
1/2 tsp smoked paprika
2 tbsp olive oil
Country bread, to serve

Heat 3 tablespoons of the oil in a large, wide and deep sauté pan, add the onion and garlic and fry them for about 5 minutes until transparent. Add the chorizo and continue to fry briefly. Stir in the diced potatoes. Pour in the stock, add the bay leaves, season and bring the mixture to the boil. Reduce the heat and cook gently until the potatoes are soft, about 12–15 minutes.

Meanwhile, blanch the greens in boiling water for 2 minutes to take off any bitterness. Drain. Remove the bay leaves from the potatoes then mash the potatoes in the broth with a potato masher so a thick chowder is formed. Add as much greens to the broth as it will support. If you want a heavy soup add more, if you want lighter add less. Simmer for a few minutes to warm through.

Mix the smoked paprika with the remaining 2 tablespoons of olive oil and swirl this red magic into the soup. Serve with chunks of hearty country bread.

beef carpaccio

aaron craze

Named after the Venetian artist Carpaccio who was known for his love of deep reds, this classic Italian starter marries the delicate flavour of thinly sliced beef with beetroot and pecorino.

serves 4

preparation time: 20 minutes
cooking time: 2 minutes

2–3 fresh rosemary sprigs,
　　leaves only
2–3 fresh thyme sprigs, leaves
　　only
A handful of fresh sage leaves
A handful of fresh oregano
　　leaves, plus extra whole
　　leaves to garnish
1–2 tbsp Dijon mustard
300–350g (10–12oz) piece of
　　beef fillet, tied with string
Salt and freshly ground black
　　pepper
2 tbsp olive oil, plus extra for
　　drizzling
1 raw beetroot (about
　　250g/9oz), peeled
Balsamic vinegar, for drizzling
About 75g (3oz) pecorino
　　cheese
1 orange, preferably a blood
　　orange, halved

Finely chop the herb leaves and spread them out evenly on a plate, reserving a little thyme for later. Spread a thin layer of mustard all over the beef, and season. Roll the beef over the herbs until it is completely covered.

Heat the olive oil in a non-stick frying pan until smoking hot. Add the beef and sear quickly on all sides, about 30 seconds on each side. Remove from the pan, roll up tightly in cling film and set aside.

Shave the beetroot into wafer-thin slices using a swivel-bladed vegetable peeler. Place in a bowl, drizzle with a little vinegar and olive oil and sprinkle with the reserved thyme. Toss gently to mix.

Using a razor-sharp knife with a long blade, slice the beef as finely as you can. You should get 16 slices to serve 4. Flatten each slice with the flat side of the knife to make the meat paper thin.

To serve, arrange the beef slices on 4 plates and sprinkle the beetroot over them. Shave over the cheese, then dress each plate with whole oregano leaves, a squeeze of orange juice, a grinding of salt and pepper and a drizzle of olive oil.

cook's note

If not serving the beef immediately, keep it in the fridge and allow it to come to room temperature for about 1 hour before slicing.

crispy fried squid

sam and eddie hart

Using a coarse semolina-like flour for your batter gives a crispy coating and prevents the squid becoming too greasy.

serves 4

preparation time: 10 minutes
cooking time: 10 minutes

Vegetable oil, for deep-frying
500g (1lb 2oz) cleaned, fresh
squid (ask your fishmonger
to do this)
About 200g (7oz) Spanish frying
flour (*farina especial para
freir*) or equal amounts of
plain flour and breadcrumbs
mixed together (about
100g/3^1/$_2$oz of each)
A generous pinch of sea salt
Lemon wedges

Preheat the oil in a deep fryer to 180°C (350°F). Rinse the squid and carefully pat dry with kitchen paper. Cut the squid into 15mm (^{5}/$_8$in) rings and set aside with the tentacles.

Tip the flour or mixed flour and breadcrumbs into a large bowl. Toss a large handful of squid in the flour to coat, gently shake off the excess then carefully add to the hot oil. Deep-fry in batches for 3 minutes or until crisp and golden.

Remove the squid and drain on kitchen paper. Repeat this, cooking the remaining squid in batches. As soon as all the squid is cooked, sprinkle with a little salt and lemon juice. Serve with the remaining lemon wedges.

langoustine cocktail

james martin

A revamped version of the classic 1970s prawn cocktail, with langoustines. Perfect for a dinner-party starter.

serves 4

preparation time: 25 minutes
cooking time: 2 minutes

1kg (2lb 4oz) fresh langoustines
1 tbsp white wine vinegar
2 egg yolks
1$\frac{1}{2}$ tsp Dijon mustard
250ml (9fl oz) vegetable oil
1 tbsp tomato ketchup
A splash of Tabasco sauce
A splash of Worcestershire
    sauce
A splash of brandy
Salt and freshly ground black
    pepper
2 Little Gem lettuce, leaves
    washed and separated

to serve:
Smoked paprika for sprinkling
Lemon wedges

Bring a large saucepan of salted water to the boil, add the langoustines, bring the water back to the boil and cook for 1–2 minutes. Drain and leave to cool, then peel and set aside.

Place the vinegar into a clean mixing bowl and whisk in the egg yolks. Add the mustard and continue to whisk. Gradually whisk in enough of the vegetable oil, starting with a few drops then adding a spoonful at a time, until the mayonnaise has emulsified and thickened. Stir in the ketchup, Tabasco, Worcestershire sauce and brandy. Season to taste.

To serve, arrange the lettuce on 4 plates and divide the cooked langoustines on top. Spoon some of the mayonnaise over, sprinkle with the smoked paprika and serve with the lemon wedges. (Any leftover mayonnaise can be kept in the fridge for 2–3 days.)

chicken and artichoke terrine

jeremy lee

This impressive dish is perfect for dinner parties: it's very easy and you can make it in advance. If you can't find lardo (cured pork fat), use streaky bacon.

serves 4–6

preparation time: 25 minutes, plus chilling

cooking time: about 1 hour, plus cooling

About 125g (4½oz) thinly sliced lardo or 250g (9oz) sliced unsmoked streaky bacon

7 large, skinned organic chicken breasts

6 freshly cooked artichoke hearts, of the larger variety

6 shallots

1 tbsp olive oil

A pinch of thyme

4 or 5 fresh tarragon leaves

1 tbsp chopped fresh flat-leaf parsley

1 glass of white wine (about 100ml/3½fl oz)

1 small glass of Madeira (about 50ml/1¾fl oz)

Salt and freshly ground black pepper

for the green bean and almond salad:

150g (5oz) fresh French beans

1 tbsp olive oil

1 tsp good red wine vinegar

1 tbsp toasted slivered or flaked almonds

1.1 litre (2 pint) ovenproof terrine with a lid

Preheat the oven to 180°C (350°F), Gas mark 4.

Use enough slices of the lardo to line the terrine so it overhangs the edges slightly.

Cut each chicken breast into 3 pieces and likewise the artichokes. Cut the remaining lardo into small pieces. Peel and finely chop the shallots then cook them in a spoonful of olive oil with the thyme, until softened. Cool this and add to the meats. Add the tarragon and parsley, wine and Madeira then the seasoning. Mix well and gently heap into the lined terrine. Fold over the lardo so the terrine is enclosed, laying a few more slices across the top to cover if necessary. Lay a sheet of parchment paper on top and then cover with the lid or foil if using a loaf tin.

Place the terrine in a bain-marie (a large, deep ovenproof container half filled with hot water) and bake for 50 minutes–1 hour or until the tip of a knife is hot when pressed to the tip of your tongue after inserting it into the terrine. Once cooked, remove the lid and leave to cool with a considerable weight laid on top. Keep for a day in the fridge before serving in slices with the green bean salad.

For the salad, cook the green beans in plenty of slightly salted water for 2–3 minutes. Cool in iced water. Mix the oil and vinegar together. Drain the beans and toss with the oil and vinegar dressing, seasoning and almonds.

scallops with cima di rapa

theo randall

Overcooked scallops can be tough and chewy, so they should be added to a hot pan for very little time. They are cooked when the flesh is just firm and slightly coloured.

serves 4

preparation time: 15 minutes
cooking time: 35 minutes

4 tbsp Puy lentils
1 garlic clove, peeled and finely
    chopped
2 tsp chopped fresh sage
1½ tsp fennel seeds
1 dried chilli
1 tbsp olive oil
2 garlic cloves, peeled and
    sliced
400g (14oz) cima di rapa or
    purple sprouting broccoli or
    cavolo nero, leaves removed
    from stalks and thick parts of
    the stalks sliced
Salt and freshly ground black
    pepper

for the scallops:
12–16 scallops in their shells
    (or buy the scallops out of
    their shells and ask your
    fishmonger for 4 cleaned
    shells)
Olive oil

to garnish:
2 tsp chopped fresh parsley
2 tsp capers, drained

Place the lentils, chopped garlic and sage in a small saucepan with enough water to cover them to twice their depth. Bring to the boil, cover and simmer for about 25 minutes or until tender. Drain if necessary and set aside.

Crush the fennel and chilli together using a pestle and mortar or spice grinder. Heat the 1 tablespoon of olive oil in a large, heavy-based frying pan and lightly fry the fennel seeds, chilli and sliced garlic for 1–2 minutes. Remove from the heat.

Meanwhile, blanch the cima di rapa stalks in a pan of boiling water for 1–2 minutes, then add the leaves and cook for a further 2 minutes. Drain and stir into the fennel seeds, chilli and garlic mix. Lightly fry for a few more minutes. Remove the cima di rapa mixture from the pan and chop finely. Put it back in the pan, add the reserved lentils and heat through with a splash of olive oil. Season to taste. Keep warm.

If using scallops in their shells, remove from the shells, trim the scallops and reserve 4 cleaned shells for serving. Rub the scallops in a little olive oil then season. Heat a large frying pan and fry the scallops for 1–2 minutes on each side until slightly caramelised and just cooked. Tip the parsley and capers into the base of the pan.

To serve, pile the cima di rapa mixture into the 4 cleaned scallop shells and top with the scallops. Garnish with the parsley and capers.

cook's note
Cima di rapa is a slightly bitter cooking green, known variously as broccoli rabe, or raab, and rapini. The leafy parts of the turnip are obtained from most varieties of turnip roots. It is excellent chopped in salads or cooked briefly and used as a colourful side dish.

asparagus and boiled eggs

tom parker bowles

The short asparagus season marks the beginning of spring. The spears can be cooked in a variety of ways: boiled, griddled or roasted. An inexpensive asparagus steaming pot will ensure perfect results as well.

serves 4   vegetarian

preparation time: 5 minutes
cooking time: 7 minutes

4 eggs
1 bunch of asparagus, ends
    trimmed
Salt

Place the eggs into a pan of boiling water and boil for 7 minutes for a soft-boiled egg.

While the eggs are boiling, steam the asparagus over a pan of boiling water or in an asparagus steamer for 3–4 minutes until tender. Season with salt.

Remove the eggs with a slotted spoon and put under running cold water to cool. Peel off the shells and halve. Serve with the asparagus.

smoked salmon blinis

amanda lamb

These delicious blinis are perfect for a party. They look impressive and are super quick and easy to prepare.

makes 12

preparation time: 15 minutes

12 ready-made blinis
100g (3¹/₂oz) sliced smoked
    salmon, snipped into small
    pieces with scissors
125ml (4fl oz) crème fraîche
¹/₂ lemon
Chopped dill or chives, to garnish

Preheat the oven to 190°C (375°F), Gas mark 5.

Arrange the blinis on a baking tray in a single layer and warm through in the oven for 5 minutes.

Transfer the blinis to a serving platter and divide the smoked salmon equally among them. Top each one with a generous dollop of crème fraîche, a squeeze of lemon juice and a sprinkling of chopped dill. Serve as soon as possible.

herb omelettes stuffed with ricotta

orlando murrin

This impressive drinks-party nibble can be made ahead of time. It can be set aside until your guests arrive and you are ready to serve them.

serves 4   vegetarian

preparation time: 20 minutes
cooking time: 10 minutes, plus
    cooling

4 eggs
A handful of fresh chives,
    roughly chopped
1 garlic clove, peeled and
    crushed
3 tbsp grated Parmesan cheese
Oil, for frying

for the filling:
A small handful of fresh basil,
    roughly chopped
A small handful of fresh flat-leaf
    parsley, roughly chopped
250g (9oz) ricotta cheese
3 tbsp freshly grated Parmesan
    cheese
Salt and freshly ground black
    pepper

For the filling, whiz all the ingredients together in a blender or food processor. Check the seasoning – it should be good and tasty. Scrape into a bowl and set aside in the fridge.

Whiz the eggs, chives, garlic and Parmesan in the blender or processor (no need to wash up first).

Heat a thin layer of oil in a medium frying pan until hot. Pour in one-third of the egg mixture and let it run to the sides of the pan. When it has set, after about 2–3 minutes, slide the omelette out and leave to cool. Repeat to make 2 more omelettes, adding a little more oil each time if necessary.

When the omelettes are cold, spread one-third of the filling over each one and roll them up neatly. Set aside on a board until ready to serve.

To serve, slice each omelette on the diagonal into 6 or 8 pieces.

broccoli and parma ham rolls

matthew fort

A great way to get kids to eat their vegetables is to wrap them in Parma ham.

serves 4

preparation time: 15 minutes
cooking time: 15 minutes

24 purple sprouting broccoli
  spears, trimmed
Salt and freshly ground black
  pepper
12 slices Parma ham or another
  cured ham
Olive oil, for drizzling
Parmesan cheese shavings

Preheat the oven to 200°C (400°F), Gas mark 6.

Cook the broccoli spears in 2 batches in a large saucepan of boiling salted water until tender, about 3–4 minutes for each batch. Drain and plunge straight into cold water. When cool, drain again and dry with kitchen paper.

Lay 2 broccoli spears on one end of a slice of Parma ham, facing the florets in opposite directions. Carefully roll the ham around the spears so the florets are showing at either end. Repeat with the remaining ingredients.

Place the rolls on a non-stick baking tray, drizzle with a little olive oil and bake for about 5 minutes or until the ham is just crisp.

To serve, splash a little olive oil over the centre of 4 plates and sit 3 rolls on top of each. Finish with Parmesan shavings and a sprinkling of pepper.

broad bean, feta and herb salad

matthew fort

If you grow your own broad beans, pick them very young and serve them raw for this dish. If you buy them, the beans will probably be older and should be cooked first.

serves 4   vegetarian

preparation time: 10 minutes
cooking time: 5 minutes

1kg (2lb 4oz) fresh broad beans
    in their pods or 400g (14oz)
    podded beans
200g (7oz) feta cheese,
    crumbled into rough cubes
1/2 lemon
Extra virgin olive oil, for drizzling
Freshly ground black pepper

to serve:
4 fresh summer savory, chervil
    or mint sprigs
Crusty bread

Pod the broad beans if necessary and cook in a pan of boiling salted water for 2–3 minutes or until tender. Drain and plunge into cold water. When cool, drain again. Meticulous cooks can squeeze the beans out of their white skins, but it is fine to leave them as they are.

Toss the feta with the broad beans in a large bowl. Squeeze over the juice from the lemon and drizzle with olive oil. Season with pepper – you shouldn't need any salt as feta is quite salty.

To serve, strip the leaves off the herb sprigs and tear them into small pieces, if you like, then scatter over the salad. Serve with crusty bread.

scallop, jerusalem artichoke and lentil salad

diana henry

This autumn salad makes an impressive dinner party starter. Add lemon juice to the water before boiling the Jerusalem artichokes to prevent discolouring.

serves 4

preparation time: 20 minutes
cooking time: 40 minutes

Olive oil, for frying
1 small onion, peeled and very
   finely chopped
1 small celery stick, very finely
   chopped
1 small carrot, peeled and very
   finely chopped
100g (3½oz) Puy lentils, rinsed
500ml (18fl oz) water
Salt and freshly ground pepper
750g (1lb 10oz) Jerusalem
   artichokes
A good squeeze of lemon juice
2 tbsp finely chopped fresh flat-
   leaf parsley
200g (7oz) streaky bacon
   rashers, cut into large pieces
125–150g (4½–5oz) baby salad
   leaves
12 scallops with their corals

for the vinaigrette:
1 tsp Dijon mustard
2 tbsp white wine vinegar
100ml (3½fl oz) extra virgin
   olive oil
Caster sugar, to taste

Heat 1 tablespoon of olive oil in a medium saucepan and gently fry the onion, celery and carrot until soft but not coloured. Add the lentils and turn to coat in the oil, then pour in the water and season to taste. Bring to the boil, reduce the heat and simmer, uncovered, for 20–30 minutes until the lentils are just tender.

Meanwhile, peel the artichokes and cook them in a large saucepan of boiling salted water to which you have added the lemon juice to prevent them from discolouring. Once they are just tender but still have a little bite, about 20–25 minutes, drain and slice into thick batons.

For the vinaigrette, use a fork to whisk the mustard in a bowl with the vinegar and extra virgin olive oil. Add sugar and seasoning to taste.

Drain the lentils well and tip into a bowl, then stir in 3 tablespoons of the vinaigrette and the parsley.

Heat 2 tablespoons of olive oil in a large frying pan and fry the artichokes and bacon until coloured and cooked through, about 10 minutes. Be careful not to cook the artichokes so much that they start to fall apart.

Toss the salad leaves, artichokes and bacon with the some of the remaining vinaigrette and divide among 4 plates, piling them up in the centre. Spoon the lentils around the outside.

Season the scallops. Heat a little olive oil in a frying pan until very hot and sear the scallops for 20–30 seconds on each side until they are lightly caramelised and just cooked through. To serve, place 3 scallops on top of each salad and drizzle with a little extra vinaigrette.

endive, gorgonzola and pear salad

giorgio locatelli

The bitter flavour of endive is often married with something sweet such as fruit or red pepper. It also has a crunchy texture which is complemented by a smooth and creamy cheese for this delicious starter.

serves 4 as a starter
vegetarian

preparation time: 30 minutes

2 heads yellow endive (chicory)
2 heads red endive (chicory)
Salt and freshly ground black
    pepper
About 5 tbsp mayonnaise
1 ripe pear, such as Comice,
    peeled, cored and thinly
    sliced (preferably on a
    mandolin)
200g (7oz) Gorgonzola cheese,
    cut into 4 slices

for the vinaigrette:
6 tbsp extra virgin olive oil
2 tbsp red wine vinegar
2 tbsp water
Salt and freshly ground
    black pepper

Cut the bases off each head of endive so that the leaves come away easily. Trim the bottom sides of each leaf diagonally so they end with a point. Thinly slice the trimmings.

For the vinaigrette, whisk all the ingredients together. Place the whole endive leaves in a bowl, season and toss with the some of the vinaigrette. Place the sliced leaves in another bowl, season and toss with more of the dressing (you may have a little dressing left over).

Using a plastic squeezy bottle, drizzle the mayonnaise on plates in a zigzag pattern. Alternatively, thin the mayonnaise down with a little water and drizzle it on with a spoon. On each of 4 plates, arrange alternate yellow and red endive leaves in a circle, with their points facing outwards to look like petals of a flower. Pile some of the trimmed leaves and pear slices in the centre, then lay a slice of Gorgonzola over the top (don't worry if it breaks up into pieces). Drizzle a little more mayonnaise over and serve immediately.

wood pigeon and baby artichoke salad

arthur potts dawson

Buy pancetta with lots of fat for this recipe. Fry it in a hot pan so that it releases its nicely flavoured oils to cook the much leaner wood pigeon. Be careful not to cook the pigeon for too long or it will become dry.

serves 4

preparation time: 15 minutes
cooking time: 25 minutes

8 baby artichokes
150g (5oz) rocket
Salt and freshly ground black
    pepper
Olive oil, for dressing
12 fine slices pancetta
12 fresh sage leaves
8 wild wood pigeon breasts

Place the artichokes in a saucepan of cold water, bring to the boil, then reduce the heat and simmer for 8 minutes or until tender. Drain and leave to cool. Remove the outer leaves and trim the stalks. Snip the tips from the remaining leaves, cut the artichokes lengthways into quarters and place them in a bowl. Add most of the rocket, leaving a little for the garnish. Season to taste, add a splash of olive oil and mix well.

Place a large frying pan over a medium–high heat until hot. Add the pancetta and sage and cook for 1–2 minutes or until the sage is crisp and the pancetta is browned on both sides; remove and set aside. Add the pigeon breasts to the pan and cook for 3 minutes on each side, then turn the heat down to low and cook for a further 1–2 minutes on each side, depending on how pink you like them. Remove from the heat and leave the breasts to rest for a few minutes.

To serve, pile the salad on to 4 serving plates and scatter the sage leaves on top. Slice the pigeon breasts at an angle and arrange over the salad with the pancetta, then garnish with the remaining rocket.

rainbow superfood salad

allegra mcevedy

Revitalise your lunchbox with this healthy and colourful salad of autumn vegetables and vitamin-packed seeds.

serves 4

preparation time: 40 minutes
cooking time: $1^1/4$–$1^1/2$ hours, plus cooling

2 raw beetroots (about 250g/9oz each), unpeeled
Salt and freshly ground black pepper
100ml ($3^1/2$fl oz) water
4 vine-ripened tomatoes, halved lengthways
Extra virgin olive oil, for drizzling and frying
1 small butternut squash (about 600g/1lb 5oz), peeled, deseeded and chopped into 3cm ($1^1/4$in) cubes
1 small head of broccoli (about 300g/10oz), cut into florets
250g (9oz) fresh peas in their pods, shelled or 60g ($2^1/2$oz) frozen peas
3 tbsp quinoa
2 garlic cloves, peeled and chopped
150g (5oz) chestnut mushrooms

Set 3 shelves in the oven and preheat the oven to 200°C (400°F), Gas mark 6.

Place a beetroot in a small roasting dish with a good sprinkling of salt and the water. Cover with foil and roast on the top shelf of the oven for $1^1/4$–$1^1/2$ hours until a knife goes easily into the beetroot.

Lay the tomatoes cut-side up on a baking tray, season with salt and drizzle with 2 tablespoons of the olive oil. Roast on the lowest shelf of the oven for 1 hour.

Place the cubes of butternut squash on another baking tray and roll them in a little olive oil and plenty of salt and pepper. Roast on the middle shelf of the oven for 45 minutes, moving the pieces around at least once.

While the vegetables are roasting, prepare the other ingredients. Bring a saucepan of lightly salted water to the boil and blanch the broccoli florets and peas for 2 minutes. Lift them out with a slotted spoon into a colander and run them under cold water until completely cooled.

Tip the quinoa into the broccoli water and stir then simmer for 15 minutes. Drain and leave to cool.

Heat a frying pan until hot, then add 1 tablespoon of olive oil and when hot, lightly fry the garlic for a moment, swiftly followed by the mushrooms. Season with salt, pepper and the lemon juice and remove them from the pan in less than 4 minutes.

2 tbsp lemon juice
100g (3¹/2oz) red cabbage,
   finely shredded
2 tbsp toasted seed mix, such
   as linseeds, sesame seeds,
   pumpkin seeds, poppy
   seeds
30g (1oz) alfalfa shoots
Dressing of your choice, to
   serve

Place the shredded cabbage in a bowl. Peel and grate the remaining raw beetroot and mix with the cabbage.

When the roasted vegetables are cooked, leave them to cool, but peel the beetroot while it is still warm and cut into chunky wedges.

To serve, layer the vegetables in a large glass bowl, starting with the quinoa on the bottom, then the cabbage and beetroot mix, followed by the broccoli and peas, squash, tomatoes and mushrooms. Finish with the toasted seeds and alfalfa shoots, season to taste and add a dressing of your choice.

spring panzanella

silvana franco

An Italian 'leftover' dish that uses day-old bread and tomatoes as the base, plus your favourite seasonal vegetables from the market.

serves 4 as a side salad
vegetarian

preparation time: 15 minutes
cooking time: 10 minutes

1 bunch of asparagus, woody
    ends snapped off
1 thick slice of sourdough
    bread
Olive oil
Salt and freshly ground black
    pepper
400g (14oz) tin cannellini beans,
    drained and rinsed
1/2 red onion, peeled and thinly
    sliced
4 ripe plum tomatoes
1 tbsp balsamic vinegar
A pinch of light muscovado
    sugar
2 fresh soft thyme sprigs,
    leaves only, torn
A large bunch of fresh flat-leaf
    parsley, leaves only, roughly
    chopped

Cook the asparagus in a pan of boiling salted water for 3 minutes.

Meanwhile, heat a griddle pan. Drizzle the bread with some olive oil then cook on the griddle for a few minutes on each side until nicely browned.

Drain the asparagus, toss in a little olive oil and salt and cook on a hot griddle for a few minutes until charred in places.

Place the beans and onion in a large bowl. Halve the tomatoes and squeeze the juice and seeds onto the beans and onion, then tear the flesh into pieces and add. Mix in some olive oil (about 3–4 tablespoons), the vinegar and sugar and stir together. Add some thyme leaves to the bowl along with some parsley. Cut each asparagus stalk into 3 pieces and add to the bowl. Tear the toasted bread into chunks and place in a serving dish.

Pour the tomato and dressing mixture over the bread. Toss well together, season and serve cool or at room temperature (not chilled).

mackerel niçoise

tana ramsay

A deliciously different take on the classic French salad. Mackerel is a healthy choice as the fish with the most Omega-3 and it's good value.

serves 4

preparation time: 15 minutes
cooking time: 25 minutes

400g (14oz) Jersey Royal
     potatoes
4 eggs
2 large handfuls of French
     beans, stem ends trimmed
2 heads of chicory, leaves
     separated
12 cherry tomatoes, halved or
     8 small plum tomatoes,
     quartered
A large handful of black olives,
     stoned
Salt and freshly ground black
     pepper
8 fresh mackerel fillets, skin on
Olive oil

for the dressing:
50ml (1^3/4fl oz) olive oil
1^1/2 tbsp white wine vinegar
1 tbsp lemon juice
Freshly ground black pepper

Boil the potatoes for 15–20 minutes until tender. When done, drain, leave to cool slightly then cut them into quarters. At the same time as the potatoes are cooking, place the eggs in a medium saucepan of boiling water and boil for 8 minutes (so that they're not too runny, or too hard). Drain, then place under cold running water to cool. Peel off the shells and slice in half.

Cook the beans in a pan of boiling water for about 2–3 minutes. Drain and refresh under cold running water. Set aside. Place the chicory leaves in a large bowl. Add the potatoes, tomatoes, olives and eggs and gently mix them all together. Season and set aside.

Mix together the oil, vinegar and lemon juice for the vinaigrette, then season to taste with pepper.

Preheat a griddle pan. Gently rub the mackerel fillets on both sides with olive oil then lay them on the hot griddle. Cook for no longer than 1–2 minutes on each side (depending on their size). You may need to cook the fillets in 2 batches.

Arrange the salad on 4 plates. Lay the beans over the top then place 2 mackerel fillets on each plate. Drizzle over the vinaigrette and serve.

vietnamese crayfish salad

rachel allen

Crayfish are freshwater crustaceans and look like small lobsters. They are perfect in salads with South Asian dressings which always contain sweet, salty, hot and sour ingredients.

serves 4

preparation time: 30 minutes

125g (4½oz) thin or medium rice noodles

75g (3oz) natural (unsalted) peanuts

350g (12oz) shelled cooked crayfish

½ cucumber, chopped

150g (5oz) radishes, trimmed and sliced

4 tbsp chopped fresh coriander leaves and stalks

for the dressing:

50g (2oz) caster sugar, or more to taste

4 tbsp fish sauce

3 tbsp lime or lemon juice

2 small fresh chillies, deseeded and finely sliced

2 garlic cloves, peeled and crushed

2 tsp finely grated fresh root ginger

Preheat the grill to medium–hot.

First make the dressing by mixing all the ingredients together in a bowl or jug. Taste and add more sugar, if you like.

Soak the noodles in a bowl of boiling water for 5 minutes until they have softened. Drain thoroughly and rinse in cold water.

Toast the peanuts under the hot grill for a few minutes, then rub off the skins in a clean tea towel. Chop the nuts roughly.

To serve, toss the noodles and dressing together in a large bowl. Add the crayfish, cucumber and radishes and toss until well mixed, then sprinkle the peanuts and coriander over the top.

seasonality
matt tebbutt

Seasonality has always been my passion. I love taking the best seasonal ingredients and creating something simple and delicious for the table.

I believe good food is not about fancy presentation. It's about taking the best and freshest produce and using the lightest of touches to bring out its full potential.

When I began working my way through some of the top kitchens in London ten years ago, this approach to cooking wasn't as prevalent as it is today. It was my time spent with the great Alastair Little, now hailed as the godfather of modern British cooking, which opened my eyes to a new and far more exciting way to cook.

I learnt from Alastair that good food isn't about using clever tricks to overdress a dish. As well as knowing what you should do, great cooking is about knowing what not to do with ingredients and what not to put on a plate – it's about letting the produce speak for itself.

It's great to see increasing numbers of chefs, who trained in the same vein as me, opening pubs and restaurants that offer a confident, seasonal and simple approach to food.

Of course, it's nothing new. Our grandmothers had no choice but to cook with the seasons. When things are in season, supply is more plentiful and therefore less expensive. And if it's locally produced, it's even cheaper. This approach is more important now than ever before, not only because of the recession, but because we're all worried about where our food comes from and the effect that its transportation has on the environment.

Growing numbers of home cooks are no longer happy to fill their trolleys with imported asparagus or raspberries. They are beginning to realise that the very best produce is often grown in Britain, right on their doorstep. Although they might have to wait a bit longer, it's worth it for the superior flavours.

At home in Monmouthshire, we are particularly lucky with the quality of the local produce. I change The Foxhunter menu daily, inspired by the changing seasons. But wherever you live in Britain you can find a whole host of small producers, working to provide us with the very best this country has to offer. I'm proud that *Market Kitchen* helps give these unsung heroes of modern farming and food a chance to promote what they do.

beef salad with crisp vegetables and watercress pesto

jun tanaka

Watercress is in season from April until October. Here Jun has made use of its distinctive peppery flavour by making a variation of the classic Italian pesto.

serves 4

preparation time: 20 minutes, plus 30 minutes chilling
cooking time: 12 minutes

for the salad:
3 large radishes, trimmed
2 celery sticks, trimmed
4 asparagus spears
2 small carrots
3 tbsp olive oil
1¹/2 tsp Dijon mustard
A handful of fresh tarragon leaves

for the peppered beef:
500g (1lb 2oz) beef fillet
Olive oil, for brushing
Salt
3 tbsp cracked black peppercorns

for the watercress pesto:
1 bunch of watercress, about 100g (3¹/2oz), leaves and thin stalks
2 tbsp freshly grated Parmesan cheese
1 tbsp pine nuts
1 garlic clove, peeled
Juice of ¹/2 lemon
100ml (3¹/2fl oz) olive oil

For the salad, using a mandolin or sharp knife, finely slice the radishes, celery and asparagus. Shave the carrots into ribbons using a vegetable peeler and place all the vegetables in a bowl of iced water. Leave for about 30 minutes to crisp up.

Preheat the oven to 200°C (400°F), Gas mark 6.

Brush the beef lightly in olive oil, then season with salt and coat in the cracked black pepper. Heat an ovenproof griddle pan to very hot, add the beef and sear on all sides. Transfer to the oven and cook for 5 minutes for very rare meat. Remove and leave to rest while you make the pesto.

Place all the pesto ingredients, except for the olive oil, in a blender then drizzle in the olive oil while the motor is still running. Combine the olive oil and mustard for the salad.

To serve, drain the salad vegetables from the iced water, pat dry with kitchen paper and dress with the olive oil mixture. Toss in the tarragon leaves. Thinly slice the beef and lay it out on a serving plate. Spoon over the watercress pesto and top with the raw salad.

main courses

spaghetti with fresh tomato and basil

laura santtini

To accentuate the sweetness of cherry tomatoes try adding sugar. Perfect for a speedy supper.

serves 4 vegetarian

preparation time: 10 minutes
cooking time: 20 minutes

3 tbsp extra virgin olive oil
2 large garlic cloves, peeled
    and thinly sliced
1kg (2lb 4oz) cherry tomatoes,
    halved
A large handful of fresh basil
    leaves, torn
2 tsp caster sugar
Salt and freshly ground black
    pepper
350–400g (12–14oz) spaghetti
25g (1oz) unsalted butter

to serve:
Fresh basil leaves or sprigs
150g (5oz) ricotta cheese,
    crumbled
Black olive tapenade

Heat the olive oil in a large non-stick frying pan and add the garlic to flavour it. Just before the garlic begins to colour, stir in the tomatoes, torn basil, sugar and seasoning to taste. Leave to simmer over a low heat for a few minutes until the tomatoes have broken down.

Bring a large saucepan of salted water to the boil and cook the pasta according to the packet instructions until just tender. Drain.

Place the butter in a large serving bowl, add the pasta and the tomato sauce and toss all together. To serve, top each serving of pasta with the extra basil, the ricotta and 1–2 teaspoons of tapenade.

spinach and ricotta gnocchi

matthew fort

If you can't get fresh spinach for this recipe, frozen is a good substitute, but make sure you squeeze all the water out before mixing with the ricotta.

serves 4

preparation time: 30 minutes, plus thawing and chilling
cooking time: about 50 minutes

350g (12oz) frozen spinach, thawed, or fresh spinach weighed when cooked, and drained then dried off in a heavy-based saucepan over a low–medium heat to remove as much moisture as possible
700g (1lb 9oz) ricotta cheese
100g (3^1/2oz) fresh Parmesan cheese, grated, plus extra to finish
Freshly grated nutmeg
Salt and freshly ground black pepper
2–3 medium eggs, beaten
Plain flour, for shaping and coating

for the tomato sauce:
2–3 tbsp olive oil
1 large onion, peeled and roughly chopped
5 garlic cloves, peeled and chopped
A handful of fresh basil leaves, roughly chopped
400g (14oz) tin chopped tomatoes
500ml (18fl oz) tomato passata

For the gnocchi, tip the spinach on to a board and chop finely. Place the ricotta in a large bowl and beat until fairly smooth. Add the spinach with the Parmesan, a large pinch of nutmeg and seasoning to taste, and stir well to mix. Beat 2 eggs, add to the mixture and stir thoroughly again – if the consistency is dry, add part or all of the third egg, but do not get the mixture too wet or it will be difficult to handle. Cover and chill in the fridge for about 1 hour.

To prepare the tomato sauce, heat the olive oil in a heavy-based saucepan over a low heat, and add the onion, garlic and basil. Cover and cook gently for 5–10 minutes, shaking the pan occasionally. Add the tomatoes, passata and seasoning to taste. Stir well, then cover and cook gently for 20 minutes, stirring occasionally.

To form the gnocchi, cover a large plate or tray with a good layer of flour. Drop a dessertspoon of the gnocchi mixture on to the flour and gently roll it into a ball shape until you can pick it up with floured hands. Repeat until you have used all of the mixture to make about 32 gnocchi then chill in the fridge for at least 1 hour or until you need them.

To cook, preheat the oven to 200°C (400°F), Gas mark 6. Bring a wide, large pan of water to a gentle boil on top of the stove, then drop 6–7 gnocchi into the water. Wait for 1–1^1/2 minutes or until the balls float to the surface, then let them cook for a further 1–1^1/2 minutes before scooping them out with a slotted spoon and leaving them to drain. Keep the gnocchi warm while you cook the remainder.

When all the gnocchi are cooked, transfer them in a single layer to a baking dish. Reheat the sauce, pour over the gnocchi and sprinkle with Parmesan. Bake for 10 minutes or until hot.

melanzane alla parmigiana

matthew fort

Violet aubergines have a lighter creamier colour than normal aubergines and are rounder, but both work well in this recipe. Slicing them thickly and cooking them in this way ensures a deliciously meaty texture.

serves 4 vegetarian

preparation time: 10 minutes, plus pressing

cooking time: 1 hour 10 minutes

2 round violet aubergines or 2 medium purple aubergines, cut into even 5cm (2in) thick slices
Salt and freshly ground black pepper
Extra virgin olive oil, for frying
1 garlic clove, peeled and finely chopped
500g (1lb 2oz) tomato passata
A bunch of fresh basil, leaves roughly torn
100g (3½oz) fresh Parmesan cheese, grated

Small ovenproof dish

Lay the aubergine slices on a chopping board. Sprinkle some salt over each slice and place another chopping board on top. Place a heavy weight on top and leave to press for 2 hours.

Meanwhile, pour 1 tablespoon of olive oil into a medium saucepan and fry the garlic until it begins to colour. Add the passata and simmer gently for about 45 minutes or until thickened, stirring occasionally. Season and leave to cool.

After the aubergine slices have been pressed, briefly rinse them in a colander, then thoroughly pat dry with kitchen paper. Heat 2–3 tablespoons olive oil in a frying pan and when it's very hot, add the slices and fry for 2–3 minutes on each side until lightly browned, adding more spoonfuls of oil as necessary during cooking and when turning the aubergines over. Drain on kitchen paper.

Preheat the oven to 200°C (400°F), Gas mark 6.

Arrange the aubergine slices in a small ovenproof dish and spoon the tomato sauce over each slice. Scatter the basil leaves then the Parmesan over the top and bake for 20 minutes. Serve hot.

courgette and caerphilly risotto cakes with courgette fries

stephen terry

This is a good way to use up leftover risotto. If you can't find Caerphilly, use your favourite local cheese to add extra flavour.

serves 4   vegetarian

preparation time: 40 minutes, plus chilling
cooking time: 1 hour 20 minutes, plus cooling

5 medium courgettes
Olive oil, for frying
1 small red onion, peeled and finely chopped
150g (5oz) Carnaroli risotto rice
500ml (18fl oz) hot chicken or vegetable stock
2 tbsp chopped fresh parsley
50g (2oz) butter, cubed
100g (3$\frac{1}{2}$oz) Caerphilly cheese
Salt and freshly ground black pepper (optional)
About 5 heaped tbsp plain flour, for dusting
About 250ml (9fl oz) whole milk, for dipping
Sunflower or groundnut oil, for deep-frying

to serve:
Pea shoots
Olive oil
Lemon juice

20cm (8in) square baking tin

Prepare the courgettes. Coarsely grate 1 courgette completely, including the seeds, and keep for the risotto. Slice the remaining 4 courgettes for the courgette fries lengthways with a mandolin using the 'shredding' blade or a very sharp knife. Take 2 long thin slices (no more than 3mm/$\frac{1}{8}$in thick) from each side of the courgette, leaving a block of seeds in the middle and grate this block. Reserve for adding to the risotto. Wrap the courgette strips in cling film and chill.

Heat a little olive oil in a large, deep, wide sauté pan, add the onion and sweat for 2 minutes so it softens but doesn't lose its colour. Add the rice and cook for 2 minutes, stirring, until the grains are opaque in colour. Gradually add the stock, ladle by ladle until each spoonful is absorbed. You don't want the risotto to be traditionally wet, so keep stirring until the rice has absorbed all of the stock but is still moist, about 20–25 minutes. Bite a grain of rice in half and make sure the centre isn't white. Add the grated courgette, the remaining seeds from the finely sliced courgettes and the parsley and cook for 2 minutes. Stir in the butter and 50g (2oz) of the cheese and taste for seasoning.

Line the baking tin with cling film so it overlaps the edges. Pour in the risotto mix and evenly spread it out. The mixture should be 2cm ($\frac{3}{4}$in) in depth. (If your tin is too big, pull the mixture to the correct depth with the cling film and dam it up with foil.) Leave on a rack to cool for 1 hour, then fold over the cling film and chill for several hours or preferably overnight.

continued

continued from previous page

Preheat the oven to 180°C (350°F), Gas mark 4.

Remove the risotto from the fridge, turn it onto a board and cut into 4 individual oblong portions.

Slice the reserved courgette strips into long matchsticks. Place the flour in a lidded container and the milk in a bowl. Dust the risotto cakes all over with the flour then briefly fry in a non-stick pan over a high heat until golden on each side, adding a little oil if necessary. Place them in an ovenproof dish and bake in the oven for 5 minutes.

Meanwhile, cook the courgette fries. Heat the oil for deep-frying to 180°C (350°F) in a large, deep, heavy-based saucepan. Dip the courgette matchsticks into the milk, shake off the excess and drop them into the flour. Shake them in the lidded container so they are well coated, then tip into a large sieve and shake off the excess flour. Deep-fry the courgette matchsticks in 2 batches for 2 minutes until golden and crisp. Remove with a slotted spoon, tip them onto kitchen paper and sprinkle with crushed salt.

Serve a handful of fries on top of each risotto cake and grate over the remaining cheese. Serve with a pile of pea shoots dressed with olive oil and lemon juice.

sweet potato falafel with aïoli

allegra mcevedy

These oven-baked falafel are a much healthier take on the traditionally deep-fried version. It is important to put the falafel in the fridge before cooking so that they do not fall apart.

serves 4   vegetarian

preparation time: 40 minutes, plus chilling

cooking time: 1–1¼ hours

2 sweet potatoes, total weight about 700g (1lb 9oz), unpeeled
2 tsp ground cumin
2 small garlic cloves, peeled and chopped
2 tsp ground coriander
A large handful of fresh coriander, chopped
1 tbsp lemon juice
150g (5oz) gram flour, plus extra if needed
Salt and freshly ground black pepper
Sesame seeds, for sprinkling

for the aïoli:
1 egg
1 egg yolk
4 garlic cloves, peeled and crushed with a pinch of salt
120ml (4fl oz) sunflower oil
200ml (7fl oz) thick Greek yogurt
Juice of ¼–½ lemon

to serve:
Flatbreads
Sliced tomatoes
Cos lettuce

Preheat the oven to 220°C (425°F), Gas mark 7, then roast the sweet potatoes whole until just tender (about 45 minutes–1 hour).

Meanwhile, make the aïoli. Using an electric mixer on medium speed, combine the egg and egg yolk with the garlic for a few minutes until pale and fluffy. Start drizzling in the sunflower oil slowly, then increase the speed once the mix begins to emulsify like mayonnaise. Once all the oil is incorporated, fold in the yogurt gently by hand and finish with lemon juice and salt to taste. Keep in a covered bowl in the fridge until ready to serve.

Remove the sweet potatoes from the oven, leave until cool enough to handle, then remove the skins and place the flesh in a large bowl with the cumin, garlic, ground and fresh coriander, lemon juice and gram flour. Season well and mash until you have a smooth mix with no large chunks. Firm up in the fridge for an hour or in the freezer for 20–30 minutes.

Preheat the oven to 220°C (425°F), Gas mark 7. Oil a baking tray. Take the falafel mix out of the fridge or freezer. It should be sticky rather than really wet (sweet potatoes vary in water content enormously), so add 1 tablespoon or so more flour if necessary.

Using a falafel scoop or 2 soup spoons, make the mixture into 16 small patties by placing a well-heaped spoonful of mix in one spoon and use the concave side of the other to shape the sides. Place the falafel on the baking tray as you make them and sprinkle sesame seeds on top. Bake for about 15 minutes or until golden brown underneath.

To serve, place the falafel pasties in warm flatbread with tomatoes, lettuce and the aïoli.

carluccio's porcini risotto

antonio carluccio

A classic dish from Piedmont in northern Italy, cooked by the Italian master himself. Brushing is recommended for cleaning fresh mushrooms but dried mushrooms should be soaked.

serves 4

preparation time: 20 minutes, plus soaking (optional)
cooking time: 30 minutes

300g (10oz) firm small fresh ceps or 300g (10oz) field or button mushrooms and 20g (^{3}/$_4$oz) dried porcini
1.5 litres (2^3/$_4$ pints) chicken or vegetable stock
1 small onion, peeled and finely chopped
2 tbsp olive oil
60g (2^1/$_2$oz) butter
300g (10oz) risotto rice
60g (2^1/$_2$oz) Parmesan cheese, freshly grated

If using ceps, gently clean them using a sharp knife and a brush (avoid washing them wherever possible).

Slice the ceps or other mushrooms if you are using them. If using dried porcini, soak them in a small bowl of warm water for 15 minutes. Drain and reserve the soaking water to add with the stock later, then chop the porcini into small pieces.

Pour the stock into a large saucepan and bring to a simmer.

Meanwhile, fry the onion in the oil and half of the butter. When the onion begins to colour, add the mushrooms and continue to fry over a medium heat for 2 minutes. Add the rice and cook for a further 1–2 minutes, stirring, until it just turns translucent.

Start to add the hot stock ladleful by ladleful, stirring all the time and letting it absorb into the rice before adding the next. If using the mushroom soaking water, you will not need all of the stock.

After about 20 minutes, when the rice is al dente, remove from the heat. Season and stir in the remaining butter and the Parmesan. Serve hot.

my obsession with food

tom parker bowles

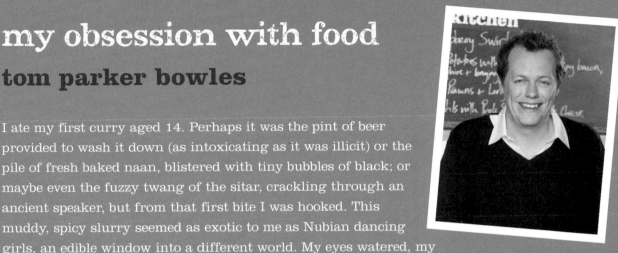

I ate my first curry aged 14. Perhaps it was the pint of beer provided to wash it down (as intoxicating as it was illicit) or the pile of fresh baked naan, blistered with tiny bubbles of black; or maybe even the fuzzy twang of the sitar, crackling through an ancient speaker, but from that first bite I was hooked. This muddy, spicy slurry seemed as exotic to me as Nubian dancing girls, an edible window into a different world. My eyes watered, my lips burnt but my taste buds rejoiced. This was food miles removed from the simple, fresh English food I grew up on.

My mother was a fine cook, my father a dedicated gardener, so there were asparagus in May, peas and broad beans in summer, and blissfully scented tomatoes from August onwards. All cut and picked within 50 metres of the kitchen. We ate grilled Dover sole and brown trout freshly hauled from the stream. There was roast beef from the local farm, eggs from our chickens and spectacular sausages from Love's, our brilliant butcher. My gastronomic upbringing was also enriched by annual jaunts to Ischia, a small island in the Bay of Naples. And my love for intense tomato sauces, ricotta and mozzarella, good pizza and gelato, endures to this day. My first taste of the subcontinent, though, was not superior to all the above, just fundamentally different.

From that moment on, my obsession with food from every corner of the globe, especially Asia and Mexico, began to shape my life. I craved the tongue-tingling hit of real Sichuan pepper, the thin, pearlescent pastry that wrapped my dim sum, the smoky depth of the chipotle chilli, and the searing heat of the fruity habanero. As I got older, I started to travel to the places I'd formerly only dreamt of, the tourist posters made real, to Laos and South Korea, New Orleans and New York, Guadalajara and Galicia.

I found a love of food cut through more barriers more quickly than a thousand stuttering Berlitz phrases. A smile and muffled 'yum' made me friends in moments, wherever I was. And a quick glance at a nation's food will give you more idea of its history, economics and anthropology than any dusty, turgid guide. To eat across the world gives one an insight into different cultures, and an appreciation too. It also provides pleasure in its most delectable form.

prawn biryani

anjum anand

Traditionally biryani is a baked dish but this recipe is all prepared on the hob and then layered onto a serving dish to make a spectacular dinner party main course.

serves 4

preparation time: 30 minutes
cooking time: 40 minutes

for the garnish:
6 tbsp milk
2 large pinches of saffron
    strands
A dash of vegetable oil
1 large onion, peeled and
    finely sliced

for the curry:
2 tsp cumin seeds
2 tsp coriander seeds
10 black peppercorns
1 cinnamon stick
4 cloves
4 green cardamom pods
2 dried red chillies
4 large garlic cloves, peeled
    and roughly chopped
5cm (2in) piece fresh root
    ginger, peeled and roughly
    chopped
400g (14oz) ripe tomatoes,
    quartered and roughly
    chopped

To prepare the garnish, heat the milk gently in a small saucepan with the saffron, then remove from the heat and leave to infuse. Heat the oil in a small frying pan, add the onion and fry over a medium–high heat for 5–7 minutes or until crisp and brown. Set aside.

To make the curry, grind the whole spices to a fine powder using a spice grinder or sturdy pestle and mortar. Make a paste of the garlic, ginger and tomatoes in an electric blender adding a little water to slacken the paste.

Heat the oil in a large, heavy-based pan, add the chopped onion and fry over a medium–high heat, stirring frequently, until golden. Add the ground spices, turmeric and salt to taste and stir. Mix well and cook over a high heat, stirring frequently, until it is reduced and the oil comes out at the sides, about 12–15 minutes.

Meanwhile, make the rice. Heat the oil in a large non-stick sauté pan or deep frying pan, add the bay leaves and whole spices and cook for 20 seconds over a medium heat. Add the rice and stir well to coat with the oil. Pour in the water and season. Stir and bring to the boil, then simmer for 2 minutes. Cover the pan tightly, reduce the heat to low and cook for 9–11 minutes or until the grains are just soft.

Add the coconut to the curry with a good splash of water. Leave on a low heat, stirring occasionally and topping up with water, if necessary.

continued

continued from previous page

5 tbsp vegetable oil
1 large onion, peeled and
    chopped
1/2 tsp turmeric
Salt and freshly ground black
    pepper
60g (2 1/2oz) creamed coconut,
    grated
20–28 raw prawns, peeled
    and deveined

for the rice:
3–4 tbsp vegetable oil
3 bay leaves
12 black peppercorns
7.5cm (3in) cinnamon stick
4 cloves
6 green cardamom pods
2 black cardamom pods
300g (10oz) basmati rice,
    washed well and drained
600ml (1 pint) water

Take the rice off the heat and leave to steam while you finish the curry. Add the prawns to the curry along with some water, if necessary: the consistency should be medium-thick. Once the prawns are pink, about 2–3 minutes, turn off the heat.

To serve, layer half of the rice in a large serving dish, top with a layer of the curry and finish with the remaining rice. Drizzle with the hot saffron milk and top with the fried onions. Using a large spoon, fold spoonfuls of the rice into the curry to mix lightly, while retaining the separate colours.

grilled mackerel with rhubarb, chilli and mint

lawrence keogh

Did you know that rhubarb is actually a vegetable not a fruit? For this dish you can use forced rhubarb in January or wild rhubarb in spring.

serves 4   vegetarian

preparation time: 10 minutes
cooking time: 20 minutes, plus cooling

1 large fresh red chilli
4 tender sticks rhubarb, cut into about 3cm (1¼in) long pieces
450ml (15fl oz) water
200g (7oz) granulated sugar
20 fresh mint leaves
2 whole mackerel, filleted and pin-boned (ask your fishmonger to do this), so you have 4 fillets
Salt and freshly ground black pepper

to serve:
Mixed salad leaves
A dash of extra virgin olive oil
A squeeze of lemon juice
Lemon wedges

Preheat the grill to high. Place the chilli under the hot grill for a few minutes until the skin is black. Remove and wrap it in cling film. When it is cool, peel and remove and discard the seeds. Finely chop the chilli and set aside.

Place the rhubarb in a large heatproof bowl. Pour the water into a small saucepan, add the sugar and bring to the boil, stirring to dissolve the sugar. Boil for 1 minute, add the chilli and pour this over the rhubarb (the heat of the stock syrup should cook the rhubarb without needing to return it to the heat). Leave to cool to room temperature, then add the mint.

Season the mackerel and grill, skin-side up, under a very hot grill without turning, for about 4 minutes until cooked, leaving it a little pink in the middle.

Dress the salad leaves with a dash of olive oil, a squeeze of lemon and some salt. Arrange the leaves in the middle of 4 plates, place the mackerel on top and garnish with the rhubarb, a little of the spiced stock syrup and a lemon wedge.

orecchiette with purple sprouting broccoli and anchovies

aaron craze

The Puglian pasta Orecchiette, or 'little ears' in Italian, are cup shaped to catch the sauce, giving the perfect balance of pasta and sauce in each mouthful.

serves 4

preparation time: 30 minutes, plus resting

cooking time: 15 minutes

600g (1lb 5oz) purple sprouting broccoli, trimmed

Salt and freshly ground black pepper

2 tbsp extra virgin olive oil, plus extra to serve

20 anchovy fillets in oil, drained and chopped

2 garlic cloves, peeled and coarsely sliced

2 medium fresh red chillies, deseeded and sliced

Grated zest of 1 lemon

100ml (3^1/2fl oz) dry white wine

A dash of lemon juice

60g (2^1/2oz) pecorino cheese, grated

for the pasta:

200g (7oz) '00' pasta flour, plus extra for dusting

200g (7oz) semolina flour

A good pinch of salt

About 180ml (6^1/2fl oz) tepid water

First make the pasta. Combine the flours and salt in a bowl. Slowly add the water, stirring at first with a wooden spoon and then gathering and kneading with your hands until the mix comes together as a pliable dough. You may need slightly less or more water depending on the absorbency of the flours.

To form the orecchiette, pinch off pieces of the dough and flatten out with your thumb. They should be roughly the size of a penny and about 3mm (^{1}/8in) thick. Dust with a little extra flour if they become too sticky and leave to dry for at least 30 minutes.

Meanwhile, slice the stalks of the broccoli crossways into short pieces. Bring a large saucepan of salted water to the boil, blanch the broccoli for 1 minute, then drain in a colander.

Refill the saucepan with salted water and bring to the boil. Drop in the pasta and cook for 8–10 minutes or until al dente.

Meanwhile, heat 2 tablespoons of olive oil in a large, deep frying or sauté pan and fry the anchovies over a medium heat for a few seconds, then add the garlic, chillies and lemon zest and fry for a further 1–2 minutes. Tip in the broccoli and toss until coated in the mixture, then pour in the wine and lemon juice. Season to taste (remember the anchovies are salty) and toss until hot and evenly mixed.

Drain the pasta, add to the broccoli mixture with the grated cheese and toss gently to combine. Drizzle with olive oil before serving.

cook's note

You can also use 300–350g (10–12oz) dried orecchiette. Cook according to the packet instructions until *al dente*.

really good fish pie

galton blackiston

Use any combination of fish for this recipe, but the secret to making this 'really good' is to keep the fish chunky.

serves 8

preparation time: 30 minutes
cooking time: 1¹/₂ hours

for the mash topping:
1.25kg (2lb 10oz) Maris Piper potatoes, peeled and chunkily chopped
A large knob of butter
4 tbsp double cream
3 egg yolks

for the filling:
200g (7oz) whole, undyed smoked haddock, with skin on
900ml (1¹/₂ pints) milk
1 fresh rosemary sprig
1 onion, peeled and sliced
200g (7oz) salmon fillet, skinned and cubed
200g (7oz) cod fillet, skinned and cubed
Olive or vegetable oil, for frying
12 king-size scallops
1 monkfish tail, membrane removed and chunkily diced
200g (7oz) cooked large prawns, peeled
3 tbsp capers, drained and rinsed
3 hard-boiled eggs, shelled and chopped

for the sauce:
125g (4¹/₂oz) butter, diced
100g (3¹/₂oz) plain flour
550ml (19fl oz) whipping cream
4 tbsp chopped flat-leaf parsley
2 tbsp lemon juice

For the topping, place the potatoes into a saucepan of cold salted water and bring to the boil. Cover and simmer for about 20 minutes or until the potatoes are very soft. Drain and leave in the colander to extract as much liquid as possible. Now mash the warm potatoes and work them through a sieve into a bowl. Beat in the butter, cream and egg yolks; check the seasoning and set aside.

For the filling, place the haddock in a shallow pan with 600ml (1 pint) of the milk, the rosemary and onion. Bring to a simmer over a medium heat and poach for 3–5 minutes or until the fish flakes easily with a fork. Remove the haddock from the milk with a slotted spoon and set aside. Repeat this poaching process in the same milk, firstly with the salmon and then with the cod. When the haddock is cool, remove the skin and flake the flesh into chunks. Strain the poaching milk into a jug, add the remaining milk and set aside.

Heat a non-stick frying pan over a high heat, add a splash of oil and quickly sear the scallops on each side, just enough to colour them. Remove from the pan. Do the same with the monkfish.

For the sauce, melt the butter in a heavy-based saucepan, add the flour and cook over a medium heat for 2 minutes to make a roux. Now pour in the milk from the jug (with the pan still on the heat), beating until you have a very thick, béchamel-type sauce. Beat in the cream and heat through, stirring. Remove from the heat, stir in the parsley, lemon juice and season to taste.

Preheat the oven to 200°C (400°F), Gas mark 6. Arrange the fish, scallops and prawns in a 2 litre (3¹/₂ pint) baking dish, layering where necessary. Pour any fish juices into the sauce and mix well, then gently fold in the capers and chopped eggs. Pour the sauce over the fish and cover with the mash. Bake for 40–45 minutes or until the mash is tinged golden brown and the filling is hot right through when pierced in the centre with a skewer.

monkfish with saffron and capers

tom aikens

Monkfish is a meaty fish and suits a number of cooking methods: roasting, pan frying, barbecuing or steaming. Here it is poached to create a luxurious sauce to serve with pasta.

serves 6

preparation time: 30 minutes
cooking time: 1 hour

for the saffron sauce:
50g (2oz) butter
300g (10oz) shallots, peeled
    and thinly sliced
500ml (18fl oz) white wine
1 litre (1 3/4 pints) fish stock
500ml (18fl oz) double cream
2 large pinches of saffron
    strands
Salt (optional)
1 tsp caster sugar
50ml (1 3/4fl oz) lemon juice

for the fish:
600–700g (1lb 5oz–1lb 9oz)
    monkfish tail, cut into pieces
25g (1oz) baby capers
1 tbsp chopped fresh basil

to serve:
Cooked spaghetti
3 plum tomatoes, deseeded
    and finely chopped

For the sauce, melt half the butter in a large saucepan and gently fry the shallots for 3–4 minutes until semi-soft. Pour in the wine, turn up the heat and reduce by two-thirds. Add the stock and reduce by another two-thirds, about 15–20 minutes, skimming off any scum that rises to the surface. Keep the sides of the pan clean or the sauce will go brown. Pour in the cream and saffron then reduce to half the volume, about 20–25 minutes. Remove from the heat.

Pour the sauce into a blender and season to taste with salt if needed, the sugar and lemon juice. Add the remaining butter and blend for 1 minute. Pass through a fine sieve into a clean large, wide sauté pan.

For the fish, bring the sauce to a simmer over a low heat. Season the monkfish pieces and poach them in the sauce until cooked through, about 6–8 minutes. Stir in the capers and basil. Serve with the spaghetti, scattered with the chopped tomatoes.

sole goujons with pea shoots and mint mushy peas

jason atherton

Japanese panko breadcrumbs give these posh fish fingers a deliciously light and crisp coating. They can be bought in Oriental food stores.

serves 4

preparation time: 30 minutes
cooking time: 10 minutes

A few fresh mint sprigs, leaves only
350g (12oz) frozen peas
1 tbsp Chardonnay vinegar or good-quality white wine vinegar
Salt and freshly ground black pepper
3–4 heaped tbsp plain flour
1 large egg
60g (2½oz) Japanese Panko breadcrumbs
600–700g (1lb 5oz–1lb 9oz) sole fillets, skin and pin-bones removed, sliced into 2cm (¾in) thick strips
Groundnut oil, for deep-frying
A large handful of pea shoots and micro leaves, to garnish
Tartare sauce, to serve

Place the mint in a pan of salted water and bring to the boil. Tip in the peas, bring the water back to the boil and cook for 2–3 minutes or until tender. Drain the peas and mint, transfer to a blender or food processor and add the vinegar. Pulse to a rough purée, adding a little boiling water as necessary to obtain the desired consistency. Season to taste and keep warm.

Tip the flour into a shallow bowl and season. Place the egg in another bowl and beat it with a fork. Scatter the breadcrumbs on a large plate. Toss the fish strips into the flour to dust evenly all over, then dip into the beaten egg and roll in the breadcrumbs to coat.

Heat a 2cm (¾in) depth of groundnut oil in a large deep-sided frying pan until hot (a piece of bread should sizzle immediately when dropped into the oil). Deep-fry the fish fingers, in batches, for 1–2 minutes on each side until golden brown and crisp. Remove and drain on kitchen paper, then sprinkle with a little more salt.

Divide the goujons and mushy peas among 4 warm plates. Garnish the peas with a few pea shoots and micro leaves and serve with a heaped spoonful of tartare sauce on the side.

glass noodles with salmon, lime and mint

jill dupleix

Cut down on your prep time by adding the herbs unchopped. Just let them wilt and soak up all the flavours.

serves 4

preparation time: 30 minutes
cooking time: 5 minutes

500g (1lb 2oz) salmon fillets
1 tbsp sweet chilli sauce
1/2 tbsp olive oil
200g (7oz) glass noodles or rice
   vermicelli
10 cherry tomatoes, quartered
1 avocado, peeled, stoned and
   roughly chopped
3 small red shallots, peeled and
   finely sliced
1 small fresh red chilli, finely
   sliced (do not deseed if you
   like it hot)
A handful of fresh mint leaves
A handful of fresh basil or Thai
   basil leaves
A handful of fresh coriander
   leaves
2 tbsp peanuts, chopped
Lime wedges, to serve

for the dressing:
2 tbsp tamarind paste or lime
   juice
2 tbsp Thai fish sauce
2 tbsp sweet chilli sauce
1 tbsp olive oil
2 tsp caster sugar

Skin the salmon fillets then coat in the sweet chilli sauce. Heat a large frying pan, add the oil and sear the salmon for 2–3 minutes on each side, leaving it a little pink in the middle. Leave to cool for 15 minutes.

Meanwhile, place the noodles in a bowl, pour on enough boiling water to cover and leave for 4 minutes. Tip into a colander or sieve and drain well. (To make them easier to eat, you can snip the soaked and drained noodles in half with scissors – and to stop them sticking together, place them briefly under running hot water and drain again.)

Whisk all the dressing ingredients together in a large bowl. Gently toss the tomatoes, avocado, shallots and chilli into the dressing, add the drained noodles and herbs and lightly toss. Be as generous with the herbs as you can. They don't need cutting as they will wilt into the salad.

Divide among 4 plates. Break up the salmon with your fingers and gently tuck into the noodles. Scatter with peanuts and serve with lime wedges for squeezing.

brill with tomato, cucumber and ginger salsa

rachel allen

The addition of ginger gives this dish an Asian twist. Mackerel can be used instead of brill as a cheaper but just as delicious alternative.

serves 4

preparation time: 25 minutes
cooking time: 20 minutes

1.75kg (3lb 14oz) whole brill, filleted (see cook's notes)
Plain flour, for coating
A large knob of butter, softened

for the salsa:
6 tbsp rice vinegar or white wine vinegar
2 tbsp fish sauce
50g (2oz) caster sugar
250g (9oz) ripe tomatoes, diced into 1cm (1/2in) pieces
1/2 cucumber, deseeded and diced into 1cm (1/2in) pieces
1 small red onion, peeled and diced
1 spring onion, trimmed and diced
1/2–1 fresh red chilli, deseeded and diced
Juice of 1/2 lime, or more to taste
2 tsp finely grated fresh root ginger, or more to taste
2 tbsp coarsely chopped fresh coriander

First make the salsa. Heat the vinegar, fish sauce and sugar together in a saucepan, stirring to dissolve the sugar. Boil for about 5 minutes or until reduced slightly. Transfer to a large bowl and leave to cool. Add the remaining salsa ingredients except the coriander and toss together well. Taste and add more lime juice or ginger if necessary, then top with the coriander. Set aside.

Now prepare the beans. Plunge them into a pan of salted boiling water and cook for 5 minutes or until tender but still quite firm. Drain. Heat the oil in a frying pan over a medium heat, add the mustard seeds and fry for 1–2 minutes until they start to pop, then add the chilli and garlic and fry for a further 2–3 minutes. Add the beans and toss together thoroughly, taste for seasoning and set aside.

Coat the 4 brill fillets in flour seasoned with salt and pepper and spread the fleshy side with softened butter. Cook buttered-side first in a very hot frying pan for 2 minutes or until golden brown underneath, then turn the fillets over and cook for 2 minutes on the other side. To serve, place the brill on 4 plates, spoon the salsa on top of the fish and the beans alongside.

for the asian green beans:

300g (10oz) fine green beans,
   trimmed

Salt and freshly ground black
   pepper

2 tbsp sunflower or vegetable
   oil

1 tsp black mustard seeds

1 fresh red chilli, deseeded
   and diced

1 garlic clove, peeled and
   finely chopped

cook's notes

Brill is sold as a whole fish and the size varies according to the season. This recipe uses 1 large fish that gives 4 large fillets, but if the brill are small you will need 2 whole fish to give 2 small fillets per person. Ask the fishmonger to fillet the fish for you and to remove the skin if you prefer it without; if the fillets are very large you may find it easier to cut them in half crossways before cooking, and to use two frying pans.

The salsa can be made up to 1 hour before serving. If you keep it longer than this the cucumber and tomatoes will make it too watery, so you will need to drain it in a sieve before serving.

harissa-spiced halibut with couscous

mark sargeant

Harissa is a fiery chilli paste from North Africa that can be both a condiment and an ingredient. Add to a marinade, stir it into stews, or mix with a little oil and serve as a dip.

serves 4

preparation time: 25 minutes, plus soaking and marinating
cooking time: 10 minutes

1 tbsp harissa paste
1 tbsp olive oil
1 tsp caster sugar
150g (5oz) natural yogurt
4 x 150g (5oz) halibut fillets, skinned
1–2 tbsp vegetable oil

for the herb couscous:
250g (9oz) couscous
300ml (10fl oz) boiling chicken or vegetable stock
1 tbsp harissa paste
2–3 tbsp ready-made vinaigrette
Large handfuls of fresh parsley, leaves chopped
Large handfuls of fresh mint, leaves chopped
Small handfuls of fresh coriander, leaves chopped
Salt and freshly ground pepper

for the cucumber salad:
2 cucumbers, peeled
A handful of fresh mint leaves, chopped
A squeeze of lime juice

Mix the harissa with the olive oil and sugar in a non-metallic dish. Add all but 3–4 tablespoons of the yogurt (reserve this for the cucumber salad) and stir well. Coat the halibut with the spiced yogurt mixture and set aside for 10 minutes. (The fish could be kept overnight in the fridge for a more intense flavour.)

For the couscous, measure the couscous into a large bowl then pour over the boiling stock and stir in the harissa. Cover with cling film and leave to soak for 10–15 minutes. Remove the cling film then fluff up the couscous with a fork to separate the grains. Stir in the vinaigrette and herbs and season to taste.

For the cucumber salad, using a swivel vegetable peeler, slice the cucumbers lengthways into long wide strips, avoiding all the seeds in the middle. Discard the central block of seeds. Place the cucumber strips in a large bowl. Mix with the mint, the reserved yogurt and the lime juice to taste.

Preheat the oven to 200°C (400°F), Gas mark 6.

Heat the vegetable oil in an ovenproof frying pan over a medium–high heat. Scrape off and reserve the excess marinade from the halibut and place the fillets in the pan. Sear for about 1–1¹/₂ minutes on each side until golden brown. Spoon the reserved marinade over the fish then transfer the pan to the oven for a few minutes to finish cooking the fish.

Serve the halibut on 4 warm plates drizzled with the pan juices, with the couscous and cucumber salad.

plaice with chickpea purée, ceps and green leaves

richard corrigan

Plaice is a delicious alternative to salmon at Christmas. It's in season during the winter months and wrapping it in cured pork fat gives it extra richness and a sense of occasion.

serves 4

preparation time: 20 minutes
cooking time: 20 minutes

12–20 slices lardo (see cook's note)
4 large plaice fillets, as thick as possible, skinned
8 fresh ceps
1–2 tbsp extra virgin olive oil, plus extra for drizzling
4 handfuls of mixed salad leaves
Lemon juice, for drizzling

for the chickpea purée:
400g (14oz) tin chickpeas, drained and rinsed
2 garlic cloves, peeled and roughly chopped
1 fresh red chilli, deseeded and roughly chopped
Juice of 1 large lemon
1 tsp ground cumin
About 7 tbsp extra virgin olive oil
Salt and freshly ground black pepper
1–2 tbsp hot water (optional)

First make the purée. Cook the chickpeas with the garlic and chilli in a saucepan of boiling water for 10 minutes. Drain, then purée in a blender or food processor until smooth with the lemon juice and cumin and 7 tablespoons of olive oil. Check for seasoning and consistency, adding more oil and the hot water if the purée is too thick.

Preheat the oven to 200°C (400°F), Gas mark 6.

Wrap 3–5 slices of lardo around each fillet to cover the fish completely (depending on the size and thickness of the fillets, you may find it easier to cut them crossways into smaller pieces first). Place the fish on a baking sheet and roast for 8 minutes. Remove from the oven and leave to rest for 5 minutes.

Meanwhile, lightly fry the ceps in the 1–2 tablespoons of olive oil.

To serve, place the fish on 4 plates with the chickpea purée and ceps. Pile the salad leaves alongside and drizzle with olive oil and lemon juice.

cook's note

Lardo is cured pork fat that is sold at Italian delicatessens. You should ask for it to be sliced in wafer-thin rashers – they will wrap around the fish easily. If you have any left over, you can serve it raw in thin slivers as part of an antipasto with bread, salami, ham and olives, etc.

red mullet with hazelnuts and fennel

angela hartnett

Fennel is in its seasonal prime during the summer, principally in July. Its aniseed flavour makes a delicious accompaniment to any oily fish for a light and tasty lunchtime meal.

serves 4

preparation time: 15 minutes
cooking time: 20 minutes

25g (1oz) butter
50g (2oz) hazelnuts, skinned
150ml (5fl oz) olive oil
2 tbsp hazelnut oil
2 tbsp white wine vinegar
Salt and freshly ground black
    pepper
8 baby fennel bulbs
8 red mullet fillets, scaled and
    pin-boned

to serve:
Lettuce
Fresh herb leaves, such as mint,
    flat-leaf parsley and basil

Heat the butter in a non-stick frying pan until bubbling, add the hazelnuts and roast over a medium heat for 2–3 minutes, constantly shaking the pan to prevent them sticking. Remove and leave to cool, then chop roughly and place in a bowl with 6 tablespoons of the olive oil, the hazelnut oil and vinegar. Mix well to combine, season to taste and set aside.

Place the fennel in a bowl, season and add 2 tablespoons of the remaining olive oil. Heat a griddle pan until hot, add the fennel and cook for 7–8 minutes, turning halfway through, until browned and tender. Remove from the heat and set aside.

Heat the remaining 2 tablespoons of olive oil in a non-stick frying pan over a medium heat, add the fish fillets, skin-side down, and cook for 3 minutes, shaking the pan to stop them sticking, until golden brown. Turn them over gently with a palette knife and cook for a further 2 minutes. Remove the fish from the pan.

To serve, mix the lettuce and herb leaves together with some of the dressing and place in small piles on 4 plates. Place 2 fennel on each plate, then 2 fish fillets, skin-side up. Spoon the remaining dressing and nuts over and around.

jamaican brown chicken stew with yard-style gravy

levi roots

This spicy chicken stew is an old family recipe and a firm favourite.

serves 4–6

preparation time: 20 minutes, plus marinating

cooking time: 35 minutes

8–10 chicken pieces, such as thigh, breast, leg, skinned
Juice of 1 lemon
1 tsp salt
2 tbsp all-purpose seasoning, such as a Caribbean everyday seasoning
1 tsp coarsely ground black pepper
2 tsp chicken seasoning or extra all-purpose seasoning
200–300ml (7–10fl oz) vegetable oil
3 spring onions, trimmed and chopped
2 onions, peeled and chopped
1 fresh Scotch bonnet chilli, deseeded and chopped
1 garlic clove, peeled and chopped
1/2 red pepper, deseeded and chopped
1/2 green pepper, deseeded and chopped
450ml (15fl oz) water
A knob of butter
Cooked basmati rice, to serve

Rub the chicken all over with the lemon juice to remove all traces of the skin. Place the chicken in a non-metallic dish and sprinkle with the salt, all-purpose seasoning, black pepper and chicken seasoning. Using your hands, rub the seasonings in to give the meat a good flavour, then cover and leave it in the refrigerator for 30 minutes or overnight if you have time. (Be sure to wash your hands really well after touching raw chicken.)

Heat the vegetable oil in a large deep flameproof casserole or sauté pan with a lid until really hot. Remove the chicken from the seasoning, reserving any seasoning mix. Carefully put 4–5 pieces of chicken into the oil and fry gently for about 5 minutes on each side until the chicken is browned. Remove the chicken from the casserole and repeat with the remaining chicken pieces. Carefully pour out most of the oil, leaving just 2 spoonfuls in the base.

Add the spring onions, onions, chilli, garlic and peppers and stir briefly. Return all the chicken to the casserole with any reserved seasoning mixture. Pour in the water, add the butter, bring to the boil then reduce the heat, cover and simmer for about 15 minutes or until the liquid is reduced to a rich gravy and the chicken cooked through. Serve with rice.

chicken korma with fragrant rice

silvana franco

Korma is a mild curry and a great way to introduce kids to spicy flavours.

serves 4

preparation time: 15 minutes
cooking time: 15 minutes

300g (10oz) basmati rice
2 bay leaves
4 cardamom pods, cracked

for the chicken:
1 tbsp vegetable oil
1 onion, peeled and sliced
2 garlic cloves, peeled and
    chopped
A small knob fresh root ginger,
    peeled and finely chopped
4 chicken breast fillets, cut into
    cubes
1 tsp garam masala
200ml (7fl oz) hot chicken or
    vegetable stock
100ml (3^1/$_2$fl oz) coconut milk
3 tbsp ground almonds
Salt and freshly ground black
    pepper

to garnish:
A handful of sliced toasted
    almonds
A handful of fresh coriander
    leaves

Half-fill a medium saucepan with water, bring to the boil and add the rice, bay leaves and cardamom pods. Return to the boil then reduce the heat and simmer for about 10 minutes until the rice is tender. Drain well.

Meanwhile, heat the oil for the chicken in a large frying pan and fry the onion, garlic and ginger for 2 minutes until softened and slightly coloured. Stir in the chicken and garam masala and cook for a further 2–3 minutes, stirring frequently, until the chicken is sealed on the outside and no longer pink.

Pour the hot stock over the chicken and simmer gently for 5–6 minutes until the chicken is cooked through. Stir in the coconut milk and ground almonds, warm through briefly, then season to taste. Serve on a bed of the fragrant rice, scattering over the almonds and coriander to garnish.

lemon chicken with roasted garlic mash

merrilees parker

If you're using whole lemons or zest, try to buy un-waxed lemons. Waxed are fine if you're just using the juice. If you can't buy un-waxed, scrubbing with a brush will remove most traces of wax.

serves 4

preparation time: 20 minutes
cooking time: 2 hours
   15 minutes

5 large baking potatoes
1 garlic bulb, unpeeled (top
   sliced off to make it easy to
   remove cooked cloves)
50g (2oz) butter
100ml (3^{1}/2fl oz) milk
^{1}/2 tsp white pepper

for the lemon chicken:
1 free-range chicken jointed
   (ensure the legs are cut into
   thighs and drumsticks)
2 tbsp light olive oil
salt
25g (1oz) butter
1 tbsp flour
2 tbsp Dijon mustard
4 tbsp Fino sherry
200ml (7fl oz) fresh chicken stock
^{1}/2 tsp white pepper
1 large unwaxed lemon, halved
   and pips removed
A generous dash of double
   cream
1–2 tsp chopped fresh flat-leaf
   parsley

Preheat the oven to 200°C (400°F), Gas mark 6. Skewer the baking potatoes and cook in the oven for about 1^{1}/2 hours, then wrap the garlic in foil and cook for a further 40 minutes.

Meanwhile, heat a wide heavy-based casserole dish. Season the chicken with plenty of salt. Add the oil to the casserole and fry the chicken pieces until they are brown all over. Remove from the casserole and rest on a plate while you make the sauce.

Add the butter to the casserole then stir in the flour. Allow to cook out for a few seconds then whisk in the mustard. Next pour in the sherry and allow the alcohol to evaporate before stirring in the stock, pepper and lemon juice. Keep stirring until smooth.

Bring to a gentle simmer then add the chicken pieces skin-side up (the pan should be wide and shallow enough so the sauce doesn't cover the chicken). Cook in the oven for 20–25 minutes until the sauce is thick and the chicken cooked through.

When the potatoes are soft and completely cooked through, remove them from the oven, slice in half and leave to cool slightly. Meanwhile, heat the butter and milk together with the pepper and a good pinch of salt. When the garlic is really soft, remove the foil and gently squeeze out the soft cloves into the milk and butter mixture.

Scoop out the flesh from the potatoes and pass through a potato ricer into a heavy-based saucepan, then fold in the garlic, butter and milk mixture, check the seasoning and keep warm. Remove the chicken from the oven and mix in the cream and parsley.

To serve, divide the mash among 4 warm plates, place the chicken on top and serve with the sauce on the side.

roast chicken with chorizo and thyme stuffing

rachel allen

The chorizo in this stuffing gives a delicious Spanish twist. Serve with mashed or roast potatoes and veg.

serves 4

preparation time: 20 minutes
cooking time: 1 hour
   50 minutes

1.5–1.75kg (3lb 5oz–3lb 14oz)
   chicken
A small knob of soft butter

for the stuffing:
25g (1oz) butter
1 onion, peeled and finely
   chopped
75g (3oz) chorizo, chopped
   into 1cm ($^1/_2$in) dice
75g (3oz) soft white
   breadcrumbs
2 tbsp chopped fresh flat-leaf
   parsley
2 generous tsp chopped fresh
   thyme
Salt and freshly ground black
   pepper

for the gravy:
350ml (12fl oz) chicken stock
1 tsp fresh thyme leaves

to serve:
Roast potatoes or mash
Seasonal vegetables

First make the stuffing. Melt the butter in a saucepan, add the onion and chorizo and cover with the lid. Cook over a low heat for 8–10 minutes until the onion is soft. Take off the heat and stir in the breadcrumbs and herbs. Season to taste and leave until cold.

Preheat the oven to 200°C (400°F), Gas mark 6. Spoon the stuffing loosely into the carcass of the chicken, making sure that it is not packed in too tightly (there should be enough room for the heat to cook the stuffing thoroughly). Place the chicken in a roasting tin and smear the soft butter over the skin, then season.

Roast the chicken for 1$^1/_2$ hours or until cooked through. The legs should feel quite loose in the bird, and the juices should run clear when a thigh is pierced with a skewer. If the chicken is getting too brown during cooking, cover it with a butter wrapper or a piece of foil or parchment paper. Once cooked, transfer the chicken to a serving plate and leave to rest in a warm place.

For the gravy, place the roasting tin over a medium heat on the stove. Pour in half of the stock and bring to the boil, whisking to dislodge the sweet juicy bits that have stuck to the tin. Pour the gravy into a French gravy boat or gravy separator and degrease in the usual way. Or pour it into a small bowl and add 2 ice cubes to draw the fat up to the top so you can spoon it off and discard.

Pour the gravy into a small pan, add the remaining stock and thyme and bring to the boil. Season, then boil to reduce if watery.

To serve, carve the chicken and serve with the stuffing, gravy, potatoes and vegetables.

lemongrass and lime chicken burgers

bill granger

These tasty Asian burgers make a great weekend lunch. If you can't find minced chicken ask your butcher to mince some for you. Serve with the Spicy Slaw on p.131, soft rolls, lettuce leaves and chilli sauce.

serves 4

preparation time: 30 minutes, plus chilling

cooking time: 8 minutes

1 small onion
1 garlic clove
1 lemongrass stalk
400g (14oz) minced chicken
60g (2½oz) fresh white breadcrumbs
2 tbsp chopped fresh coriander
2 tsp finely grated lime zest
1 tbsp fish sauce
2 tsp caster sugar
Light-flavoured oil, such as rapeseed, for brushing

Peel and finely grate the onion and peel and crush the garlic. Finely chop the white part of the lemongrass, then place with the chicken, onion, breadcrumbs, garlic, coriander, lime zest, fish sauce and sugar in a large bowl and mix well with your hands. Shape into 4 patties, cover and chill for at least 30 minutes.

Heat a barbecue or griddle pan until hot. Brush the burgers with a little oil and cook for 4 minutes on each side or until cooked through. Serve the burgers in soft rolls with lettuce, mint, coriander and chilli sauce.

cook's note

If you can't find minced chicken at the supermarket, ask your butcher to mince whole skinless chicken breasts for you. You will need 2–3 breasts to get 400g (14oz) mince.

cheesy roast chicken breasts with tomato concasse

galton blackiston

This summery dish uses chicken crowns, or chicken fronts, where the legs have been removed from the bird and the breasts left on the bone. Your butcher can prepare them for you.

serves 4

preparation time: 25 minutes
cooking time: 40 minutes

100g (3½oz) full-fat soft cheese
25g (1oz) butter, softened
1 tbsp chopped flat-leaf parsley
1 tbsp snipped fresh chives
1 tbsp chopped fresh mint
1 tbsp chopped fresh tarragon
1 tbsp chopped fresh chervil
2 garlic cloves, peeled and finely
    chopped
Grated zest of ½ lemon
Salt and freshly ground black
    pepper
2 small chicken crowns from
    two whole chickens weighing
    1.5–1.75kg (3lb 5oz–3lb
    14oz) each

for the tomato concasse:
2 large shallots, peeled and
    finely sliced
1 garlic clove
500g (1lb 2oz) plum tomatoes
4 tbsp olive oil
2 tbsp shredded fresh basil

Preheat the oven to 200°C (400°F), Gas mark 6.

Place the cheese and butter in a bowl with the chopped herbs, garlic, lemon zest and seasoning to taste. Beat together well.

Loosen the skin of the chicken away from the breast meat with your fingertips and carefully spread the cheese mixture between the skin and the flesh, trying not to break the skin. Place the crowns in a roasting tin and season well. Roast for 40 minutes until they are nice and golden and cooked through.

While the chicken is roasting, make the tomato concasse. Peel and finely slice the shallots then smash, peel and purée the garlic. Set aside. Using a sharp knife, remove the cores from the tomatoes and score a cross in the bottom of each one. Place them in a bowl and cover with boiling water, leave for 20 seconds, then remove and quickly peel off the skins. Quarter the tomatoes, remove the seeds and roughly dice the flesh.

Heat the oil gently in a saucepan, add the shallots and garlic and fry over a low heat for about 5 minutes until softened. Add the tomatoes, season to taste and heat through gently.

Remove the chicken from the oven and leave to rest for a few minutes before carving. To serve, stir the basil into the tomato concasse and divide equally among 4 warm plates. Arrange the carved chicken on top.

one-pot tarragon chicken

tana ramsay

Using one pot to cook an entire meal means that as the ingredients simmer, all the flavours blend together. This casserole can be served with vegetables, pasta or rice, or with a salad for something lighter.

serves 4

preparation time: 30 minutes
cooking time: 55 minutes

Olive oil, for frying
1 medium-sized chicken, jointed into 8 pieces
16 shallots, peeled
6 garlic cloves, peeled and thinly sliced
50ml (1³/4fl oz) tarragon vinegar
150ml (5fl oz) vermouth
1/2 chicken stock cube dissolved in 250ml (9fl oz) boiling water
100ml (3¹/2fl oz) half-fat crème fraîche
25g (1oz) fresh tarragon, leaves only and roughly chopped
Freshly ground black pepper

Heat 1 tablespoon of olive oil in a large, deep frying or sauté pan with a lid, add the chicken, in batches if necessary, and brown on all sides over a medium heat, adding more oil if needed. Transfer to a plate and set aside.

Drizzle a bit more oil into the pan if necessary, then fry the shallots until they start to colour. Add the garlic and fry until both are golden. Increase the heat and add the vinegar and vermouth, scraping the base of the pan to deglaze it. Let the liquid reduce until about half of it remains. Return the chicken to the pan, pour in the stock and bring to the boil. Reduce the heat to a simmer, cover and cook for 20–25 minutes, then increase the heat and cook, uncovered, for a further 15 minutes to create a sauce and finish cooking the chicken.

Remove from the heat and place the chicken in a warm serving dish. Stir the crème fraîche and half the tarragon into the sauce and season to taste with pepper. To serve, pour the sauce over the chicken and sprinkle with the remaining tarragon.

quick and easy bang bang chicken

tana ramsay

This dish of Chinese street food traditionally gets its name from the banging sound of the mallet that's used to shred the chicken.

**serves 2 as a main or
4 as a starter**

preparation time: 15 minutes
cooking time: 2 minutes

250g (9oz) smooth or crunchy
    peanut butter (with added
    sugar)
2 tbsp water
2 tbsp sweet chilli sauce
2 tbsp toasted sesame oil
1 tsp vegetable oil
2 carrots, peeled and cut into
    long shreds
3 spring onions, trimmed and
    cut into long shreds
1/2 cucumber, deseeded and
    cut into long shreds
2 tbsp rice vinegar
3 skinless, boneless chicken
    breasts, cooked and
    shredded
4 tsp toasted sesame seeds

Spoon the peanut butter into a heatproof bowl, add the water, chilli sauce and both oils and stir through. Sit the bowl over a saucepan of boiling water until it warms and softens to a thick, spoonable consistency.

Place the carrots, spring onions and cucumber in a bowl and stir through the vinegar. Arrange on a serving plate, place the shredded chicken on top and generously spoon over the peanut sauce. Finish by sprinkling over the sesame seeds.

cook's note
Tana poaches her chicken breasts in simmering water or chicken stock for about 20 minutes until cooked through.

duck breasts with fig balsamic vinegar

matthew fort

There is a natural empathy between duck and figs and this is the perfect way to use fig balsamic vinegar. You can use normal balsamic vinegar as a substitute.

serves 4

preparation time: 20 minutes
cooking time: 50 minutes

4 large duck breasts
16 bay leaves
Salt and freshly ground black pepper
4 tbsp fig balsamic vinegar
Olive oil, for frying
8 fresh figs, roughly chopped or sliced
4 fresh duck livers
1 whole raw beetroot (about 250g/9oz), peeled and thinly sliced with a mandolin or vegetable peeler

Preheat the oven to 150°C (300°F), Gas mark 2.

Carefully remove the skin from the duck flesh, leaving it attached at one end. Place 4 bay leaves on each breast and cover with the skin, pressing it down well. Season the skin. Place the duck breasts skin-side down on a roasting tray, season the flesh and drizzle over half of the vinegar. Roast the duck for 45 minutes, turning the breasts over halfway so that they are skin-side up. Leave to rest for 10 minutes.

Meanwhile, heat a little olive oil in a frying pan until hot and fry the duck livers for a few minutes until just cooked through.

To serve, pile the figs on 4 plates, place the livers on top and the beetroot around them. Slice the duck breasts and arrange over the livers, then drizzle with the juices and remaining vinegar.

venison steaks with smashed celeriac and carrots

aaron craze

A hearty winter dish that's best made during the venison season which runs from September to February.

serves 4

preparation time: 30 minutes, plus marinating and resting
cooking time: 40 minutes

4 venison steaks, weighing about 130g (4$\frac{1}{2}$oz) each
Grated zest of 1 large orange
3 garlic cloves, peeled and crushed
3 fresh rosemary sprigs
Olive oil, to cover
3 tbsp water
3 tbsp red wine
50g (2oz) butter, diced
A splash of balsamic vinegar

for the vegetables:
1 large head celeriac (about 750g/1lb 10oz), peeled and cut into 1cm ($\frac{1}{2}$in) cubes
3 tbsp olive oil
50g (2oz) butter, diced
1 glass of dry white wine
Grated zest and juice of 1 large orange

Place the venison steaks in a single layer in a non-reactive container with the orange zest, garlic and rosemary. Add enough olive oil to just cover the steaks, then cover and leave to marinate in the fridge for 24–48 hours.

When ready to cook and serve, remove the venison from the fridge and allow to come to room temperature for 1–2 hours.

Prepare the vegetables. Sauté the celeriac in a hot pan with 1 tablespoon of the olive oil until coloured on all sides, about 10 minutes. Add the butter and wait until it has melted, then pour in the white wine and add the orange zest and half of the juice. Sprinkle in the thyme leaves and season to taste. Add a splash of water to cover the celeriac if necessary, then press a disc of greaseproof paper over the celeriac and cook for 5–6 minutes or until the cubes are soft when pierced with a fork. Remove the paper and reduce the liquid a little before taking off the heat and smashing the celeriac with a potato masher or fork. Stir in the extra virgin olive oil and parsley. Set aside.

Preheat the oven to 220°C (425°F), Gas mark 7.

Place the carrots in a saucepan of cold water and bring to the boil. Cook for about 10 minutes or until just tender. Drain and place in an ovenproof dish with the remaining 2 tablespoons of olive oil, a good pinch of salt and the remaining orange juice. Place the dish in the oven.

continued

continued from previous page

A few fresh thyme sprigs,
    leaves only
Salt and freshly ground black
    pepper
1 tbsp extra virgin olive oil
1 tbsp chopped fresh flat-leaf
    parsley
6 carrots, washed or scrubbed
    with the peel left on and
    quartered lengthways

Now remove the venison from the marinade and season the meat. Sear on a hot griddle pan for 1 minute on each side to colour all over, then transfer to a shallow ovenproof pan. Add the water, red wine and half of the butter and finish cooking in the oven for 8 minutes.

Remove the steaks from the oven and leave to rest on a board while you finish the dish. Place the venison pan on top of the stove and reduce the juices by half, then add the remaining butter and a splash of vinegar to make a sauce. Reheat the celeriac on top of the stove and remove the glazed carrots from the oven.

To serve, pile the celeriac onto 4 warm plates and arrange the carrots around. Slice the venison and place on top, then drizzle with the sauce.

pot roast pheasant with bacon and herb mushrooms

matt tebbutt

Pheasant is a nice alternative to chicken during the winter months when it is in season and cooking it as part of a pot roast is a good way to keep the meat moist.

serves 4

preparation time: 25 minutes,
   plus marinating
cooking time: 50 minutes

50g (2oz) butter
2 pheasants
1 white onion, peeled and cut
   into 1cm (1/2in) dice
2 celery sticks, trimmed and cut
   into 1cm (1/2in) dice
1 head garlic, unpeeled and
   halved widthways
50g (2oz) smoked bacon, diced
200ml (7fl oz) dry white wine
200ml (7fl oz) double cream
2 bay leaves
3 fresh thyme sprigs

for the mushrooms:
2 handfuls of large field
   mushrooms
Olive oil, to cover
Salt and freshly ground pepper
2 shallots, peeled and finely
   chopped
1 garlic clove, peeled and crushed
A handful of Japanese Panko
   breadcrumbs, toasted
A small handful of fresh flat-leaf
   parsley, chopped
A small handful of fresh tarragon,
   chopped

First marinate the mushrooms. Slice them into thirds and place in a bowl, then cover with olive oil and season. Leave to marinate for 1 hour.

Preheat the oven to 200°C (400°F), Gas mark 6.

Heat the butter in a large ovenproof casserole dish. Season the pheasants and brown on all sides. Remove from the casserole and set aside.

Place the onion, celery, garlic and bacon into the casserole and fry gently for about 10 minutes until the onion has softened and the bacon has released its fat. Add the wine, cream and herbs and bring to the boil. Return the pheasants to the casserole and cover with the lid. Cook in the oven for 25–30 minutes or until the meat has cooked through, then remove from the oven and leave the birds to rest in the sauce for 10 minutes.

Meanwhile, remove the mushrooms from the oil and shake off the excess. Heat a frying pan until hot, add the mushrooms and cook for a few minutes until starting to turn golden, then add the shallots, garlic, breadcrumbs and herbs. Cook for 1 minute or until the breadcrumbs have absorbed all the oil from the mushrooms, then season to taste.

To serve, lift the pheasants out of the sauce and carve into joints, then return to the sauce and warm through if necessary. Serve hot with the mushrooms alongside.

pork fillet with mustard crust

giorgio locatelli

Mustard fruits are whole candied fruits preserved in a mustard-flavoured syrup and are well worth seeking out from an Italian delicatessen.

serves 4

preparation time: 25 minutes, plus soaking and freezing
cooking time: 1 hour 40 minutes

160g (5¹/₂oz) dried borlotti beans
3 garlic cloves
1 celery stick, sliced
2 fresh sage sprigs
1 bay leaf
2 tbsp extra virgin olive oil, plus extra for drizzling
Salt and freshly ground black pepper
2 tbsp tomato passata
A handful of fresh flat-leaf parsley, chopped

for the pork and crust:
150g (5oz) mostarda di frutta (Italian mustard fruits)
About 50g (2oz) fresh white breadcrumbs
25g (1oz) butter, softened
850g (1lb 14oz) pork fillet, sliced into 4 equal pieces
8 thin slices pancetta
2 tbsp sunflower or vegetable oil

Soak the beans overnight in a large bowl in plenty of cold water.

Rinse the soaked beans in a colander, then place them with the whole garlic cloves, celery, sage, bay leaf and the 2 tablespoons of olive oil in a pan and cover with plenty of cold water (about double the volume of the beans). Cover with a lid and bring to the boil. Remove the lid, skim the foam from the top and reduce the heat to a gentle simmer. Cook gently for about 45 minutes–1 hour until the beans are soft to the bite. At this point, take the pan off the heat, add salt to taste then leave the beans to cool in their cooking liquid.

While the beans are cooking, place the mostarda di frutta for the crust into a food processor and process until finely chopped. Add enough of the breadcrumbs, followed by the butter, so everything comes together in a paste. Chill in the freezer for up to 30 minutes.

Meanwhile, blanch the broccoli in a pan of boiling salted water for 2 minutes. Drain and set aside.

Take the mostarda di frutta mixture from the freezer. Lay a sheet of parchment paper on the work surface. Spoon over the mixture and put another sheet of parchment paper on top. Roll over it with a rolling pin until the mixture has flattened out into an oblong just a few millimetres thick. Put back in the freezer.

Meanwhile, preheat the oven to 250°C (475°F), Gas mark 9.

Cut each piece of pork in half widthways and wrap each one in a strip of pancetta. Secure the pancetta in place with string. Heat a large ovenproof frying pan until medium-hot. Pour in the sunflower

200g (7oz) broccoli florets
3 tbsp olive oil
1 garlic clove, peeled and
    chopped
1 fresh green chilli, deseeded
    and chopped

oil, season the pork with pepper and add to the pan. Fry for 2 minutes on each side until golden, making sure you keep the heat high otherwise the meat will 'boil' rather than brown. You may need to cook the pork in 2 batches. Transfer the pork to the oven (if you don't have an ovenproof frying pan, transfer them to a roasting tin). Cook for about 3 minutes then leave to rest.

Take the crust from the freezer and, working very fast (as it will soften up almost straight away), cut out 8 pieces, roughly the same size and shape as each piece of pork. Return to the freezer for a few minutes to harden again.

Lift the beans from their cooking water and put in a separate pan. Add a ladle or two of the cooking water to the beans and the passata (the beans should be quite soupy). Warm through and season to taste. Keep warm.

Take the crust from the freezer, lift each piece with a fish slice and lay on top of each piece of pork. Return to the oven for 5 minutes. Preheat the grill.

Meanwhile, place the 3 tablespoons of olive oil in a frying pan, add the chopped garlic and chilli and fry for a few minutes until the garlic starts to colour. Add the broccoli and season. Toss around for 2 minutes then reduce the heat.

Take the pork out of the oven and put it under the grill (if you have a combined oven/grill, turn your grill to high and, as soon as it is hot, put the pork underneath). Grill until the crust becomes light golden, taking care not to let it burn.

Stir the chopped parsley into the beans and spoon onto warm plates. Drizzle with olive oil and arrange the broccoli around the plate. Take the pork from under the grill, remove the strings and sit the meat on top of the beans.

ham hock, mustard fruits and fresh herb sauce

matt tebbutt

Ham hocks need long, slow cooking so that the meat becomes tender but it's certainly worth the wait. They are good value for money too, so perfect for a family meal.

serves 4–6

preparation time: 35 minutes

cooking time: 2 hours
  45 minutes, plus cooling

2 salted gammon hocks, about
  1.5kg (3lb 5oz) each
4 celery sticks, trimmed and cut
  in 3 widthways
3 carrots, peeled and halved
  lengthways
2 white onions, peeled and halved
1 garlic bulb, unpeeled and
  halved widthways
1 bay leaf sprig
A handful of fresh parsley stalks
3 fresh thyme sprigs
3 cloves
1 tsp black peppercorns
About 100g (3¹/₂oz) mostarda di
  cremona (Italian mustard fruits)
  from a jar or bottle, sliced or
  chopped if large, to serve

for the fresh herb sauce:
A small bunch of fresh tarragon,
  mint, basil and flat-leaf parsley
1 tbsp red wine vinegar
1 tbsp Dijon mustard
Extra virgin olive oil
1 tbsp capers, drained
1 red onion, peeled and diced

To remove excess salt, place the hocks in a very large saucepan, add cold water to cover and bring to the boil for 1 minute. Scoop off any scum then remove the hocks and change the water. Cover them again in cold water in the pan and repeat the process twice more.

Cover the hocks with fresh water in the pan, throw in the vegetables along with the garlic and all the herbs and spices, then bring to the boil. Reduce the heat and simmer for about 2–2¹/₂ hours or until the small bone at the top of the hocks can be pulled free. Remove from the heat and allow the hocks to sit in the stock until they are cool enough to handle.

For the sauce, wash and chop the tarragon, mint, basil and parsley. Whisk the vinegar, mustard and about 6 tablespoons of extra virgin olive oil together in a bowl. Stir in the herbs, capers and onion. Season and add more olive oil to bind if necessary. Allow to mingle at room temperature for a while to improve the flavours.

When the hams are cool enough to handle, remove them from the stock, trim off the outer layers of rind and fat, then pick over the meat to remove any more fat or sinew. Keep the meat in nice big chunks, do not shred. Set aside.

Strain the ham cooking liquor through a fine-meshed sieve. Pour 800–900ml (1¹/₂ pints) of it into a medium saucepan and boil to reduce by about half, about 15 minutes, to concentrate the flavours. (It can be cooled and kept in the fridge until required.)

When ready to serve, simply heat the reduced stock and put the ham in it. Simmer for a few minutes and serve with some mostarda di cremona and a spoonful of the herb sauce.

sausages with beer and onion gravy

matthew fort

Give an extra kick to your onion gravy by adding a good slug of beer from any bottle you have to hand. A delicious Saturday night supper, served with best ever creamy mash.

serves 4

preparation time: 15 minutes
cooking time: 1¼ hours

8–12 pork sausages
2 tbsp vegetable oil
1 Savoy cabbage
    (500–600g/1lb 2oz–1lb 5oz),
    cored, shredded and
    washed
A large knob of butter
Salt and freshly ground black
    pepper

for the onions:
2 tbsp pork or duck fat or
    butter
3 large onions, peeled and
    sliced
500ml (18fl oz) beer (see cook's
    note)
1 star anise
A bunch of fresh thyme

Start with the onions. Melt the fat or butter in a heavy-based flameproof casserole on top of the stove until smoking hot. Toss in the onions and fry until beginning to soften. Pour in the beer and add the star anise. Simmer for 50–60 minutes, stirring frequently, until the liquid reduces to a wonderful oniony, beery glop.

Meanwhile, gently fry the sausages in the oil in a heavy-based frying pan for about 45 minutes, turning once. Alternatively, for a healthier option, roast at 150°C (300°F), Gas mark 2 for 45 minutes.

When the onions are done, remove from the heat and add the thyme. Leave to infuse while you stir-fry the cabbage with the butter and seasoning until tender, about 5 minutes. Serve the sausages hot with the onions and buttered cabbage.

cook's note
You can use your favourite beer, lager or stout, as long as it isn't bitter. Fuller's Honey Dew, Coniston Bluebird and Young's Waggledance are all good choices.

pork belly with silky mash and pak choi

jason atherton

This recipe uses a mix of European and Asian ingredients to create a delicious sweet sauce. Slow cooking will break down the fat on the pork and make it succulent and tender.

serves 4

preparation time: about 40 minutes, plus marinating
cooking time: about 4 hours

1kg (2lb 4oz) piece pork belly
About 750ml (1¼ pints) veal and/or good-quality chicken stock (not too salty)
Sautéed pak choi, to serve

for the marinade:
150ml (5fl oz) soy sauce
250ml (9fl oz) port
250ml (9fl oz) red wine
150g (5oz) light muscovado sugar
100ml (3½fl oz) sherry
150g (5oz) runny honey
3 onions, peeled and chopped
2 carrots, peeled and chopped
1 leek, trimmed and chopped
2 celery sticks, trimmed and chopped
4 coriander seeds
4 peppercorns
2 bay leaves
25g (1oz) fresh thyme
2 star anise

Rinse the pork in cold water and pat dry with kitchen paper. Combine all the ingredients for the marinade. Lay the pork flat in a large, deep casserole dish, pour over the marinade, cover and refrigerate overnight.

Lift the pork from the marinade, scraping off the bits of vegetable. Strain the marinade into a large saucepan, keeping the vegetable bits to one side. Bring the marinade to the boil then boil to reduce the liquid by half, about 20–25 minutes, skimming off any froth that rises to the surface. Leave to cool slightly.

Meanwhile, preheat the oven to 180°C (350°F), Gas mark 4.

Heat a large frying pan until hot, add the pork belly and brown for about 3 minutes on each side. Put the pork back in the casserole dish, laying it down flat. Pour the reduced marinade over the pork, baste it well, then tip over the vegetable bits. Pour in enough stock to cover, stir then cover with a lid or foil. Braise in the oven for about 2¼–2½ hours or until very tender.

Leave the pork to rest in the stock-marinade for 30 minutes. Take the pork out, let it drain, then place on a chopping board or in a shallow dish. Cover and chill for 30 minutes so it's easier to slice. Strain the stock-marinade into a large sauté pan (discard the vegetable bits) and boil until it is reduced by half to two-thirds or until thickened to a sauce-like glaze, about 20–25 minutes. Set aside.

For the silky mash:

750g (1lb 10oz) even-sized whole La Ratte or Charlotte potatoes in their skins

55ml ($1^3/4$fl oz) milk

55ml ($1^3/4$fl oz) double cream

250g (9oz) butter, cut into pieces

Salt and freshly ground black pepper

While the pork is resting, place the potatoes in a pan of salted water and bring to the boil. Reduce the heat and simmer for 20–30 minutes until they are tender when pierced with a knife. Drain well. Wearing rubber gloves to protect your hands, quickly peel the skins off the potatoes while they are still hot, using a small knife. Mash the potatoes with a potato ricer, if you have one, then push them through a sieve to get a really smooth result.

Warm the milk and cream in another saucepan. Put the potatoes back into their pan over a medium–low heat, add the butter, a little at a time, and stir in until melted. (The mash will become quite greasy at this stage but don't worry.) Stir in the hot milk and cream until the mash comes together. Season well and take the pan off the heat. The mash will be very smooth, soft and creamy. For a silky smooth result, push the mash through a fine sieve once again. Keep warm.

Warm the sauce. Cut the pork into chunky cubes or slices and return it to the sauce to heat through. Serve with the creamy mash and sautéed pak choi with a little of the reduced glaze spooned over.

cold rolled pork with basil, pine nuts and parsley

paul rankin

This is a good alternative to the Sunday roast for the summer months. You can ask your butcher to prepare the boned and skinned loin of pork for you.

cuts into about 12 slices

preparation time: 30 minutes, plus marinating
cooking time: 1 hour 20 minutes, plus cooling

1kg (2lb 4oz) boneless loin of pork, untied and skin removed
2 garlic cloves, peeled and crushed
1 tsp granulated sugar
Salt and freshly ground black pepper
1 tbsp chopped fresh basil
2 tbsp vegetable oil

for the stuffing:
200g (7oz) sausage meat
2 tbsp toasted pine nuts
2 tbsp chopped fresh flat-leaf parsley
2 tbsp chopped fresh basil
1 garlic clove, peeled and chopped

Lay the pork fat-side down on a board with one of the short edges facing you. With a sharp knife, make an incision along the length of the loin about 2cm (3/4in) in from the right-hand edge. Roll back the cut edge and cut through the thickness of the meat, working towards the left-hand edge but not cutting right through (you need to be able to open the joint out like the pages of a book). Make 2–3 diagonal slits in each 'page' to help the meat sit flat and allow the seasonings to penetrate.

Rub the meat with the crushed garlic, sugar and pepper to taste followed by the basil. Cover with cling film and place in the fridge overnight.

The next day, make the stuffing. Mix the sausage meat with the pine nuts, herbs and garlic together in a bowl. Remove the pork from the fridge and wipe off the basil with kitchen paper. Spread the sausage mixture over the inside of the pork, and season to taste. Fold the left-hand side of the pork back over the right-hand side, then roll the pork up tightly. Wrap tightly in foil, twisting the ends so that the loin is shaped into a cylinder. Leave for an hour to allow the meat to come to room temperature before cooking.

Preheat the oven to 220°C (425°F), Gas mark 7.

for the potato salad:
500g (1lb 2oz) new potatoes
125g (4¹/₂oz) shelled peas
2 tbsp white wine vinegar
2 tbsp extra virgin olive oil
1 tbsp chopped fresh chives
1 tbsp chopped fresh dill
2–3 tsp grated horseradish, to
    taste

Heat the oil in a large roasting tin over a medium–high heat on top of the stove. Place the wrapped pork in the hot oil and cook for about 2 minutes on each side, turning it carefully. Now transfer the tin to the oven and roast the pork for 10 minutes. Reduce the oven temperature to 180°C (350°F), Gas mark 4 and roast for a further 35 minutes, turning occasionally.

Leave the pork to cool, then overwrap tightly with cling film and set aside until serving time. Store in the fridge if keeping overnight, but allow to come to room temperature before serving.

For the salad, cook the potatoes in a pan of boiling salted water until tender, about 15–20 minutes. Drain well and season while still warm. Cook the peas in a separate pan of boiling salted water for 5 minutes or until tender, then drain and mix with the potatoes. Add the remaining salad ingredients with seasoning to taste and toss together until evenly mixed.

To serve, unwrap the pork and carve into even slices. Serve cold with the potato salad.

pork loin wrapped in coppa di parma

theo randall

Coppa di Parma is a herb-flavoured rolled and cured ham – buy it sliced – but this recipe would work equally well with Parma ham or pancetta. A good dish for the weekend.

serves 4

preparation time: 1 hour
cooking time: 1 hour 5 minutes

for the salsa d'herbe:
50g (2oz) ciabatta, crusts off
20g (³/4oz) fresh flat-leaf parsley
15g (¹/2oz) fresh mint leaves
15g (¹/2oz) fresh basil leaves
10g (¹/8oz) fresh marjoram or
   oregano leaves
15g (¹/2oz) wild rocket
2 anchovy fillets, ground to paste
20g (³/4oz) capers, finely chopped
1 garlic clove, peeled and
   chopped
1 tsp Dijon mustard
1 tsp red wine vinegar
50ml (1³/4fl oz) olive oil
Salt and freshly ground pepper

for the pork:
1 rosemary sprig, leaves chopped
Finely grated zest of 1 lemon
30g (1oz) unsalted butter, softened
1kg (2lb 4oz) boned pork loin,
   trimmed of skin and half its fat
120g (4¹/2oz) coppa di Parma
Olive oil, for frying
125ml (4fl oz) sweet white wine

for the roasted radicchio:
4 radicchio, quartered
2 tbsp olive oil

For the salsa d'herbe, soak the ciabatta in enough cold water to just cover it. Finely chop the herbs and rocket, in batches if necessary, then combine with the anchovies, capers and garlic. Lift out the soaked ciabatta with your hand and squeeze well to remove all the water. Mix into the herbs. In a small bowl, whisk the mustard, vinegar and olive oil until amalgamated. Season then stir this into the salsa herb mixture. Set aside until needed. The flavour improves as it stands.

For the pork, preheat the oven to 210°C (410°F), Gas mark 6¹/2.

Combine the rosemary, lemon zest and butter into a soft paste and spread the mixture all over the pork. Lay the coppa di Parma slices out on a sheet of parchment paper, slightly overlapping. Place the pork on one end and roll the paper around it so the pork is wrapped in the ham. Remove the paper, tie the pork with string to hold the coppa di Parma wrapping in place and season. Heat a splash of olive oil in a small roasting tin on top of the stove and seal the pork on one side for 2 minutes. Turn the loin over and cover with parchment paper, then roast in the oven for 55 minutes–1 hour or until done.

After the meat has been in for 50 minutes, lay the radicchio quarters in an ovenproof dish, drizzle with the olive oil and season to taste. Roast for about 15 minutes.

Lift the pork out of the tin onto a board or plate and leave to rest. Pour off any fat from the tin. Pour the wine into the tin and stir over a medium heat to deglaze it. Simmer for 5 minutes until reduced by about half. Return the pork to the pan and baste with the juices for at least 2 minutes. Serve sliced with the radicchio and salsa.

penne amatriciana

tom parker bowles

This simple spicy pasta dish is perfect when having friends round for dinner during the week.

serves 4

preparation time: 15 minutes
cooking time: 3 hours
    30 minutes

A splash of olive oil
About 500g (1lb 2oz) piece or
    thickly sliced smoked
    pancetta, sliced into
    matchstick-sized pieces
3 red onions, peeled and
    chopped
2–3 small Italian dried chilli
    peppers, crumbled
A handful of chopped fresh
    rosemary
125ml (4fl oz) red wine
4 x 400g (14oz) tins chopped
    tomatoes
400g (14oz) penne pasta
4 handfuls of freshly grated
    Parmesan cheese
Freshly ground black pepper

Heat the olive oil in a very large saucepan and fry the pancetta over a high heat for 6–8 minutes or until crisp. Add the onions and gently fry, stirring occasionally, until soft, about 15 minutes. Stir in the chilli peppers and rosemary and cook for 1–2 minutes. Pour in the wine and turn up the heat to high, cooking until the alcohol has evaporated. Stir then add the chopped tomatoes.

Reduce the heat to low and allow the sauce to simmer gently, uncovered, for about 3 hours, stirring occasionally, until the mixture has reduced right down to a very thick sauce.

When ready to serve, cook the penne in a pan of boiling salted water until al dente, about 10 minutes.

Stir 3 handfuls of the Parmesan into the sauce and cook for a further 1 minute. Drain the pasta then mix with the sauce and season with pepper. Serve on plates and scatter over the rest of the Parmesan.

gammon with irish whiskey caramel sauce

rachel allen

The whiskey caramel sauce can be made several days in advance and keeps almost indefinitely.

serves 4

preparation time: 30 minutes
cooking time: 2 hours

1.5kg (3lb 5oz) piece of gammon
About 30 cloves
150g (5oz) light soft brown
    sugar
Juice of 1 orange
Fresh flat-leaf parsley sprigs,
    to garnish

for the Irish whiskey sauce:
225g (8oz) granulated sugar
75ml (3fl oz) cold water
225ml (8fl oz) hot water
3–4 tbsp Irish whiskey

**for the pea and spring onion
    champ:**
1kg (2lb 4oz) Maris Piper
    potatoes, scrubbed
50g (2oz) butter
200ml (7fl oz) milk (or if you want
    it really rich, use three-quarters
    milk and one-quarter cream)
300g (10oz) shelled peas
50g (2oz) spring onions, trimmed
    and chopped
3 tbsp chopped fresh flat-leaf
    parsley

First make the sauce. Place the sugar and cold water in a heavy-based saucepan and bring slowly to the boil, stirring to dissolve the sugar. Boil until the sugar caramelises and becomes a deep golden colour, swirling the pan to keep the colour even (do not stir or it will crystallise). Once the sugar has caramelised, add the hot water carefully (it may spit), then boil again for a few minutes to mix with the caramel. Leave to cool for a minute or so before adding the whiskey.

Place the gammon in a saucepan of cold water and bring to the boil, then pour off the water. Fill the pan with fresh cold water, bring to the boil and drain again. If there seems to be salt floating on the surface, repeat again. If not, continue to boil for $1\frac{1}{2}$ hours or until the gammon is cooked and tender when pierced in the thickest part with a skewer.

Meanwhile, cook the potatoes for the champ in a large pan of boiling salted water for 5–10 minutes until just tender. Drain off three-quarters of the water and continue to cook over a low heat until fully cooked, about a further 20 minutes. Avoid stabbing the potatoes with a knife – floury potatoes will break up if you do. Once the potatoes are cooked, drain off the water and leave until just cool enough to handle.

Preheat the oven to 250°C (475°F), Gas mark 8.

Remove the gammon from the water and peel off the rind, leaving the fat attached. Score the fat into diamonds and stud each diamond with a clove. Mix the brown sugar and just enough orange juice to make a paste then spread over the fat. Place the gammon in a baking dish and cook in the oven for 15–20 minutes or until the fat is deep golden and glazed, basting after 10 minutes.

Meanwhile, peel the potatoes while they are still hot and mash with most of the butter. Boil the milk in a saucepan with the peas and spring onions for 4–5 minutes or until the peas are tender. Add the parsley and take off the heat, then beat into the potatoes, keeping some of the milk back in case you do not need it all. Season to taste and beat until creamy and smooth.

Leave the gammon to rest while you reheat the sauce and the champ. If necessary, add the remaining milk to the champ and beat well to mix.

To serve, carve the gammon into thick slices and place on 4 warm plates. Spoon over the sauce and serve with the champ that has the remaining butter melting in the centre.

lamb pilaf

diana henry

The combination of fruit and meat might sound unusual but the addition of dried figs, cherries and pomegranates gives a delicious taste of the Middle East.

serves 4

preparation time: 20 minutes
cooking time: 30 minutes

2 tbsp olive oil, plus extra for drizzling
400g (14oz) boneless lamb neck or loin fillet, cubed
1 onion, peeled and roughly chopped
2 garlic cloves, peeled and crushed
1 fresh red chilli, deseeded and finely sliced
1 tsp ground allspice
50g (2oz) dried sour cherries
50g (2oz) dried figs, chopped if large
300g (10oz) basmati rice
900ml (1½ pints) hot lamb stock
Salt and freshly ground black pepper

to serve:
2 tbsp chopped fresh flat-leaf parsley or mint or a mixture of both
40g (1¾oz) shelled unsalted pistachio nuts, roughly chopped
60g (2½oz) feta cheese, crumbled
½ pomegranate, seeds only
Greek yogurt, to serve

Heat the olive oil in a deep sauté pan or flameproof casserole dish over a medium–high heat and sear the lamb for about 5 minutes until browned on all sides. Add the onion, reduce the heat and fry until soft and golden. Stir in the garlic, chilli and allspice and cook for a further 3 minutes, then stir in the cherries and figs.

Add the rice and stir briefly to mix with the other ingredients. Pour in the stock and season to taste. Bring to the boil over a high heat and stir once, then immediately reduce the heat to a gentle simmer. Now cover the pan tightly and cook for 20 minutes until the liquid has been absorbed and the rice is tender. Do not stir the rice during this time.

To serve, gently fold the herbs through the pilaf with the pistachios and most of the feta. Pile the pilaf onto 4 warm plates and sprinkle over the pomegranate seeds and the remaining feta. Drizzle over a little olive oil and serve with yogurt on the side.

lancashire hotpot

matthew fort

Kidneys are an essential ingredient for this famous dish. Make sure you peel off the membrane and cut out the core when preparing them.

serves 4

preparation time: 20 minutes
cooking time: $2^{1}/_{2}$–$2^{3}/_{4}$ hours

40g ($1^{1}/_{2}$oz) dripping, plus a little melted dripping for brushing
8 lamb or mutton middle neck or shoulder chops on the bone, trimmed of excess fat
2 large onions, peeled and finely sliced
750g–1kg (1lb 10oz–2lb 4oz) potatoes, peeled and sliced
4 lambs' kidneys, sliced
Salt and freshly ground black pepper
500ml (18fl oz) lamb or chicken stock

Melt the dripping in a frying pan over a medium–high heat and brown the chops on both sides. Remove and set aside. Reduce the heat slightly, add the onions and fry in the dripping for about 10 minutes until soft.

Meanwhile, preheat the oven to 190°C (375°F), Gas mark 5.

In a large casserole dish, place a layer of potatoes, then a layer each of chops, onions and kidney slices. Season and repeat until all the ingredients are used up, finishing with a layer of potatoes. Pour in the stock, then brush the top layer of potatoes with a little melted dripping.

Cover the casserole with foil and then the lid. Cook in the oven for 2 hours. Remove the lid and foil and cook for a further 20–30 minutes or until the top is brown and crisp. Serve.

italian shepherd's pie

gino d'acampo

This classic British dish is given an appetizing Italian makeover using basil and grated Parmesan. Make sure you grate the cheese yourself as pre-grated Parmesan can dry out and lose its flavour.

serves 6

preparation time: 30 minutes
cooking time: 1 hour
    40 minutes

5 tbsp olive oil, plus extra for
    drizzling
1 large onion, peeled and finely
    chopped
3 carrots, peeled and chopped
500g (1lb 2oz) minced lamb
70g (3oz) button mushrooms,
    halved
120ml (4fl oz) dry red wine
400g (14oz) tin chopped
    tomatoes
6 fresh basil leaves, roughly
    chopped
Salt and freshly ground black
    pepper
700g (1lb 9oz) sweet potatoes,
    peeled and chopped into
    chunks
30g (1oz) salted butter
50ml (1³⁄4 fl oz) milk
150g (5oz) fresh Parmesan
    cheese, grated

28 x 20cm (11 x 8in) or similar-
    sized ovenproof casserole
    dish

Heat the olive oil in a large saucepan and fry the onion and carrots for 10 minutes or until softened.

Drizzle a small amount of olive oil over the minced lamb and mix well (this will separate any clumps), and add to the pan with the onion and carrots. Stir-fry over a high heat to brown the meat all over, separating any clumps of meat with a wooden spoon. Stir in the mushrooms and stir frequently for 5 minutes.

Pour in the wine, then reduce the heat to medium and leave to simmer for 10 minutes, stirring occasionally, until the alcohol has evaporated. Add the tomatoes and basil then season. Continue to cook, uncovered, over a medium heat for 30 minutes, stirring occasionally.

Preheat the oven to 220°C (425°F), Gas mark 7.

Meanwhile, cook the sweet potatoes in a pan of boiling salted water for 10–15 minutes or until tender. Drain, then return to the pan and mash, stirring in the butter, milk and 100g (3¹⁄2oz) of the Parmesan. Season to taste, then stir vigorously with a wooden spoon over a low heat for 2–3 minutes or until the mash is smooth and creamy.

Pour the lamb mixture into the ovenproof casserole dish and carefully spread over the mashed sweet potato, ensuring that the meat is completely covered. Sprinkle over the remaining Parmesan. Place the dish on a baking sheet and bake for 15–20 minutes or until the topping is crisp and golden brown.

moussaka

sophie grigson

This classic Greek dish traditionally uses kefalotiri cheese, but you can mix Gruyère and Parmesan for equally delicious results.

serves 6

preparation time: 30 minutes, plus salting

cooking time: 1 hour 50 minutes

3 large or 4 medium aubergines, sliced lengthways

Extra virgin olive oil

60g (2½oz) grated kefalotiri cheese or a mixture of Gruyère and Parmesan cheese

½ generous tsp ground cinnamon

for the meat sauce:

3 tbsp extra virgin olive oil

1 large onion, peeled and chopped

2 garlic cloves, peeled and chopped

450g (1lb) minced lamb

1 generous glass dry white wine (about 150ml/5fl oz)

2 tablespoons tomato purée

450g (1lb) tomatoes, peeled and roughly chopped

To make the meat sauce, heat the oil in a large saucepan or sauté pan, add the onion and garlic and cook gently until tender, without browning. Add the lamb and stir-fry until it loses its raw look. Now add all the remaining meat sauce ingredients, except the parsley, and season. Simmer for 20–30 minutes until thick, then stir in the parsley.

Sprinkle the aubergine slices with salt and leave them on boards or trays for at least 30 minutes, preferably a full hour.

Next, make the white sauce. Melt the butter in a medium saucepan and stir in the flour. Keep stirring for about 1 minute. Draw the pan off the heat and gradually add the milk, stirring it in well. Once you've incorporated about one-third of it, increase the amount you add each time. Return to a gentle heat and let it simmer for a good 10–15 minutes, stirring frequently, until it is fairly thick. Remove from the heat, stir in the cheese and salt and pepper. If not using immediately, spear a knob of butter on a fork and rub over the surface to prevent a skin forming. Reheat the white sauce gently when needed. Just before using, beat the egg and yolk into the sauce.

Preheat the oven to 190°C (375°F), Gas mark 5.

Wipe the aubergines clean with kitchen paper and lay them on oiled baking sheets, brush quite generously with olive oil and bake for about 20 minutes until tender and patched with brown. Reduce the oven temperature to 180°C (350°F), Gas mark 4.

1 tsp caster or granulated
   sugar
1¹/₂ tsp ground cinnamon
1 tbsp dried oregano
3 tbsp chopped fresh parsley
Salt and freshly ground black
   pepper

for the white sauce:
60g (2¹/₂oz) butter, plus extra
   knob (optional)
60g (2¹/₂oz) plain flour
600ml (1 pint) milk
60g (2¹/₂oz) grated kefalotiri
   cheese or mixed Gruyère
   and Parmesan cheese
1 egg
1 egg yolk

30 x 20cm (12 x 8in) or 25 x
   25cm (10 x 10in)
   rectangular or square
   ovenproof dish

Oil the ovenproof dish lightly. Lay half the aubergine slices on the base, overlapping if necessary, then spread half the meat sauce on top. Repeat these layers, then spoon over the white sauce, covering the meat entirely. Sprinkle over the grated cheese and the cinnamon. Bake for 50–60 minutes until nicely browned. Let it settle, out of the oven, for 5 minutes before cutting into squares and serving.

lamb kebabs with cumin and coriander

rachel allen

Marinating the lamb in yogurt makes it deliciously tender.

serves 4

preparation time: 25 minutes, plus marinating

cooking time: 10 minutes

450g (1lb) shoulder or leg of lamb off the bone, fat removed

150g (5oz) natural yogurt

1 tsp ground coriander

1 tsp ground cumin

A pinch of black pepper

Juice of 1/2 lemon

Salt and freshly ground black pepper

Several metal skewers or wooden satay sticks, soaked in water for an hour to prevent them catching fire

for the cucumber and tomato raita:

250g (9oz) Greek yogurt

1/2 cucumber, deseeded and finely diced

4 tomatoes or 16 cherry tomatoes, chopped

2 tbsp chopped fresh coriander or mint

1 tsp ground cumin seeds

Cut the lamb into 3cm (1 1/4 in) chunks. Mix together the natural yogurt, coriander, cumin, black pepper and lemon juice in a medium bowl. Place the lamb in the marinade, mix well and leave to stand for at least 1 hour.

While the meat is marinating, make the raita. Mix the Greek yogurt, cucumber, tomatoes, coriander and cumin together. Season to taste and chill until ready to serve.

When you are ready to cook the lamb, take it out of the marinade and season, but do not wipe it clean. Thread the meat onto the skewers. Grill on a barbecue for 8–10 minutes or use a heated griddle pan until cooked, turning and brushing them with the marinade every so often. Serve with the raita.

devon spring lamb in herb and anchovy butter

john burton race

Lamb and anchovies may not seem like a natural marriage but the saltiness of the fish seasons the meat perfectly. Serve with salad leaves and minted new potatoes.

serves 6

preparation time: 25 minutes
cooking time: 20 minutes

for the tarragon vinaigrette:
1 tbsp lemon juice
60ml (2fl oz) white wine vinegar
A pinch of caster sugar
Salt and freshly ground pepper
250ml (9fl oz) olive oil
1 garlic clove, peeled and halved
2 fresh tarragon sprigs

for the lamb:
6 boneless lamb chumps
Olive oil, for frying

for the herb and anchovy butter:
250g (9oz) unsalted butter, diced
2 shallots, peeled and diced
2 garlic cloves, peeled and finely
  chopped
2 tbsp white wine
1 fresh thyme sprig, leaves only,
  finely chopped
1/2 bay leaf, finely chopped
30g (1oz) fresh parsley, chopped
1 tsp capers, finely chopped
3 gherkins, finely chopped
2 anchovy fillets, finely chopped
6 tarragon leaves, chopped
2 egg yolks
Juice of 1/2 lemon

Place the lemon juice, vinegar, sugar and a pinch of salt and pepper for the vinaigrette into a bowl. Whisk in the olive oil gradually. Using a funnel if necessary, transfer the dressing to a jar or bottle and add the garlic and tarragon. Put a lid on the bottle or jar and leave for the flavours to infuse.

Cut the lamb chumps into 2 lengthways pieces and season. Heat a little olive oil in a heavy-based frying pan until hot then sear the lamb briefly until it is golden brown on each side. Leave to cool.

For the herb and anchovy butter, melt 20g (^{3}/4oz) of the butter in a small pan and cook the shallots and garlic until soft and translucent. Add the wine and reduce by half, then add the thyme and bay leaf and cook for a further 2 minutes. Leave to cool.

Place the rest of the butter into a food processor and process until it turns white and fluffy. Add the parsley, capers, gherkins, anchovies, tarragon, egg yolks and lemon juice and process briefly to mix, then add the cooled shallot mixture and combine. If necessary, put in the freezer to firm up.

When ready to serve, preheat the grill to medium–hot. Spread the cooked lamb liberally with the herb and anchovy butter (you won't need it all) and grill gently for 6–8 minutes. Shake the vinaigrette well and use the desired amount to dress the salad. Place the leftover butter on a sheet of greaseproof paper, roll up into a sausage and freeze for future use.

To serve, arrange the grilled lamb on a plate and serve with a dressed salad and minted new potatoes.

my love of food
amanda lamb

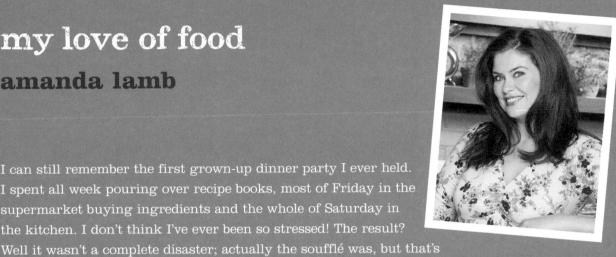

I can still remember the first grown-up dinner party I ever held.
I spent all week pouring over recipe books, most of Friday in the
supermarket buying ingredients and the whole of Saturday in
the kitchen. I don't think I've ever been so stressed! The result?
Well it wasn't a complete disaster; actually the soufflé was, but that's
another story. It really wasn't worth the amount of panic I put myself through and if I'm
really honest it did put me off experimenting with food for quite some time.

My love of food returned when I started travelling. I noticed that food in other countries
was kept simple; it wasn't so much about creating really fancy dishes, but putting
together wonderful meals using fresh ingredients. Food is the focal point of family life
and any celebration wouldn't be complete without a wonderful meal. I was lucky enough
to be in Greece during the Easter celebrations one year. Lucky for me, not so lucky if
you're a lamb! Lamb is the main ingredient eaten there and every household apparently
gets through a whole one each! I had the most delicious meal of slow-roasted lamb,
traditional Greek salad and potatoes cooked in the lamb juice flavoured with rosemary.
Now every time I smell rosemary it transports me back to that wonderful Greek island.

I think for me the country that gets it right every time is Italy. I have an apartment in
Puglia and look forward to going back time and time again. Italians love their food, but
it's all about keeping it simple and looking for the best possible ingredients you can find
and afford. That's the kind of cooking that appeals to me. If you're like me, my advice is
to cook like an Italian – keep it simple, keep it fresh and eat lots of it!

Market Kitchen has been one of the best jobs I've ever had. Getting the opportunity to
work alongside some of the best chefs in the country and learn from them has been
incredible. I continue to be amazed at the dishes they come up with. There are so many
easy to cook, affordable recipes in the show that one of the main things I've learnt from
the chefs is not to be afraid of food. Now I go home brimming with ideas. Experimenting
is all part of the fun. Sometimes it works for me, sometimes it doesn't, but now I no
longer feel the fear.

chilli beef and pepper stir-fry

ching-he huang

Before stir-frying prepare all your ingredients. Once the wok gets hot everything will cook very quickly.

serves 4

preparation time: 15 minutes
cooking time: 10 minutes

400g (14oz) fillet steak, cut into strips
2 tbsp cornflour
3 tbsp groundnut oil
5cm (2in) piece fresh root ginger, peeled and grated
1–2 fresh red chillies, deseeded and finely chopped
2–3 garlic cloves, peeled and sliced
2 red peppers, deseeded and cut into chunks
Freshly ground black pepper
2 tsp dark soy sauce
2 tbsp light soy sauce
2 tbsp hot vegetable stock
1 tsp sesame oil

Toss the strips of beef in the cornflour and set aside.

Heat a wok over a high heat until hot. Add 2 tablespoons of the groundnut oil and heat until smoking hot, then add the ginger, chillies and garlic and stir quickly for a few seconds so they do not burn. Now add the beef and stir-fry for a few minutes until browned. Transfer the contents of the wok to a plate with a slotted spoon and set aside.

Heat the remaining 1 tablespoon of groundnut oil in the wok, add the red peppers and a little black pepper and stir-fry over a medium heat for 4–5 minutes or until the peppers soften slightly.

Return the beef to the wok and stir to mix with the peppers. Finally, pour in both soy sauces and the stock and sprinkle with the sesame oil. Stir over a high heat until bubbling, then serve.

the ultimate steak sandwich

arthur potts dawson

This steak sandwich tastes great with grain mustard, ketchup, mayonnaise, sweet chilli sauce and horseradish. If you don't have a barbecue, cook your steak on a hot griddle pan instead.

serves 2

preparation time: 10 minutes
cooking time: 10 minutes

1 long ciabatta loaf
2 rib eye steaks
Olive oil, for brushing
Salt and freshly ground black
　pepper
1 tsp capers, drained
1/2 white onion, peeled and very
　finely sliced
2 medium gherkins, finely sliced
4–6 piquillo peppers (from a jar),
　drained and roughly chopped
Choice of grain mustard, tomato
　ketchup, mayonnaise, sweet
　chilli sauce and horseradish,
　to serve

Get your barbecue ready for cooking.

Place the loaf on the barbecue to quickly warm through. Remove when lightly coloured on each side.

Brush the steaks on one side with a little olive oil and season to taste. Place the steaks, seasoned-side down, on the barbecue and oil and season the unseasoned side. Turn the steaks after 3–4 minutes and cook for a further 3–4 minutes, depending on how you like your steaks cooked. Remove the steaks from the heat and let them rest for 2 minutes.

Meanwhile, slice the ciabatta in half lengthways through its thickness and sprinkle the capers over one side of the opened-out bread. Add the onion followed by the gherkins and peppers.

To serve, slice the steaks and spread out evenly over the peppers. Top with whichever sauce you like, close the ciabatta and slice in half down the middle.

perfect roast beef

matt tebbutt

There's nothing better on a Sunday than roast beef. For best results buy sirloin on the bone.

serves 6–8

preparation time: 30 minutes,
 plus marinating and resting
cooking time: 1¾–2 hours

3kg (6lb 10oz) beef sirloin on the
 bone, chined
2 garlic cloves
2 fresh thyme sprigs, leaves only
Salt and freshly ground pepper
Olive oil

for the horseradish cream:
A knob of unsalted butter
½ small onion
1 small garlic clove
125ml (4fl oz) dry white wine
4 tbsp chicken stock
125ml (4fl oz) double cream
125ml (4fl oz) crème fraîche
40g (1½oz) grated horseradish

for the gravy:
1 garlic clove
A dash of port
125ml (4fl oz) red wine
1 fresh thyme sprig, leaves only
150ml (5fl oz) beef stock

to serve:
Roast potatoes
Seasonal greens

Weigh the beef and calculate the cooking time, allowing 12–15 minutes per 450g (1lb) according to how you like your meat done. A 3kg (6lb 10oz) joint should take 1 hour 20 minutes to 1 hour 40 minutes, plus 30 minutes resting after roasting.

For the beef, peel and finely chop the garlic. Place the joint in a large bowl and rub the meat with the garlic and thyme and a generous amount of pepper and olive oil. Cover with cling film and leave to marinate in the fridge overnight or for up to 2 days if possible.

Take the beef out of the fridge 1–2 hours before roasting, to allow it to come to room temperature.

To make the horseradish cream, peel and finely chop the onion and peel and crush the garlic. Melt the butter in a saucepan until frothing and sweat the onion and garlic for 3–4 minutes or until softened but not browned. Add the wine and bring to the boil, then cook until the liquid has reduced by half. Pour in the stock and reduce by half again, then stir in the cream and let it bubble and thicken for a few minutes. Strain the sauce through a sieve into a bowl and stir in the crème fraîche. Add the horseradish and seasoning to taste and set aside.

Preheat the oven to 200°C (400°F), Gas mark 6.

Heat a large heavy-based roasting tin on top of the stove until smoking hot. Season the beef with salt and sear the joint until browned on the fat and meat sides, about 2–3 minutes on each side. Spoon the marinade over the meat then roast for 15 minutes. Reduce the oven temperature to 180°C (350°F), Gas mark 4 and roast for the remainder of the calculated time. Transfer the meat to a warm plate, cover with foil and leave to rest for 30 minutes. Reserve the cooking juices in the tin.

After the beef has rested, take the meat off the bones in one piece and reserve the bones. Keep the meat warm while you make the gravy.

For the gravy, peel and crush the garlic and set aside. Pour off all but about 2 tablespoons of the roasting juices from the tin then place the tin over a medium heat on top of the stove. Add the port and wine and bubble until reduced slightly, then add the beef bones and stir in the thyme, garlic and stock. Reduce by about half, then lift out the bones and strain the gravy into a gravy boat.

To serve, carve the meat into thick slices and place on warm plates. Spoon the horseradish cream to the side and serve with the gravy, roast potatoes and greens.

cook's notes
The horseradish cream can be made the day before and kept in the fridge overnight; it will firm up on chilling.

To check the doneness of the meat you can use a meat thermometer at the end of the calculated time. For rare meat, it should register 60°C (140°F) when inserted into the thickest part of the meat away from the bones.

slow-cooked beef stroganoff

rachel allen

This is a great dinner party main course because you can make it a whole day in advance then relax and enjoy the company of your guests. Serve with kale pilaf on page 143.

serves 4

preparation time: 15 minutes
cooking time: 2¹/₂–3 hours

for the beef stroganoff:
About 4 tbsp olive oil
500g (1lb 5oz) mushrooms, sliced
1.5kg (3lb 5oz) stewing beef, cut into 3cm (1¹/₄in) cubes
350ml (12fl oz) beef stock
3 onions, peeled and sliced
2 garlic cloves, peeled and crushed
150ml (5fl oz) dry white wine
100ml (3¹/₂fl oz) brandy
Salt and freshly ground black pepper
300ml (10fl oz) double cream

for the beurre manié:
3 tbsp butter, softened
3 tbsp plain flour

Preheat the oven to 150°C (300 F), Gas mark 3.

Heat 2 tablespoons of olive oil in a large ovenproof casserole and lightly fry the mushrooms in batches until pale golden. Tip onto a plate and set aside. Brown the meat in the same pan in small batches, adding more oil as necessary and removing each batch from the pan. Now fry the onions until softened and lightly coloured, adding the garlic towards the end and using a little more oil, if necessary.

Pour 150ml (5fl oz) of the stock into the pan and bring to the boil, stirring to deglaze. Return the mushrooms and meat to the pan, then pour in the wine, brandy and remaining stock. Add seasoning to taste, stir well and bring to a simmer. Cover with the lid, transfer to the oven and cook for 2–2¹/₂ hours or until the meat is tender.

Make the beurre manié by putting the butter and flour onto a plate and mixing to a paste. Set aside.

When the meat is cooked, carefully strain the cooking liquid into a saucepan. Keep the meat and mushrooms warm in the covered casserole. Pour the cream into the cooking liquid and boil, uncovered, for a few minutes until the sauce has reduced slightly and has a good flavour. Adjust the seasoning to taste, if necessary.

With the liquid still boiling, add the beurre manié 1 teaspoon at a time and whisk vigorously until the sauce thickens slightly. Now pour the sauce over the meat and mushrooms and stir gently to mix. Keep the warm until you are ready to serve.

pasta with bolognese sauce

gennaro contaldo

This recipe for Italy's most famous dish is unusual because it uses red wine and stock for the sauce and no tomatoes. It tastes even better the following day, when the flavours have developed.

serves 4

preparation time: 10 minutes
cooking time: 1 1/2 hours

150ml (5fl oz) extra virgin olive oil
1 onion, peeled and finely chopped
1 celery stick, trimmed and finely chopped
300g (10oz) minced beef
300g (10oz) minced pork
250ml (9fl oz) medium red wine
1 fresh rosemary sprig
Salt and freshly ground black pepper
6 tbsp tomato purée
1 litre (1 3/4 pints) hot chicken or vegetable stock
300g (10oz) fresh or dried tagliatelle
Freshly grated Parmesan cheese, to serve (optional)

Heat the olive oil in a medium saucepan, add the onion and celery and fry over a low heat for 1–2 minutes or until translucent. Stir in the beef and pork, turn up the heat and fry until the meat is brown all over, pressing out any lumps with a wooden spoon. Pour in the wine and allow to evaporate by half.

Add the rosemary, season to taste and stir in the tomato purée. Cook for 1 minute before pouring in the stock. Bring to the boil, reduce the heat and simmer gently for 1 1/4 hours, checking and stirring occasionally, adding a little hot water, if in need of extra liquid.

When the Bolognese is almost ready, prepare the pasta. Bring a large saucepan of lightly salted water to the boil, add the pasta and cook until al dente. Fresh pasta cooks very quickly in about 1–2 minutes; for dried pasta follow the packet instructions.

Drain the pasta and mix with about half of the sauce in a large bowl. Divide equally among 4 warm bowls or plates, then top each serving with an equal amount of the remaining sauce. Serve immediately with some freshly grated Parmesan, if you like.

mexican beef stew

tom parker bowles

As Mexican food has increased in popularity, ingredients have become much easier to source. Dried chipotle chillies are now available in supermarkets and online, and add a medium–hot, smoky intensity to food. If you find fresh ones, they work well here too.

serves 4

preparation time: 15 minutes, plus soaking

cooking time: 2 hours

1–3 dried chipotle chillies, to taste (see cook's note)
4 tbsp vegetable oil
1kg (2lb 4oz) chuck or braising steak, cut into 5cm (2in) cubes
1 large onion, peeled and finely chopped
2 garlic cloves, peeled and finely chopped
350ml (12fl oz) tomato passata
1 tbsp red wine vinegar
2 tsp chopped fresh oregano leaves
1 bay leaf
Salt and freshly ground black pepper
Boiled rice, to serve

Pour hot water over the chillies in a bowl and leave to soak for 30 minutes or until soft, turning them over halfway so they soak on both sides. Drain, then cut off the stems and slit the chillies open. Remove the seeds and veins before chopping the chillies finely.

Heat half of the oil in a large saucepan or flameproof casserole over a high heat until hot. Brown half of the meat for 8–10 minutes, then remove and repeat with the remaining oil and meat. Add the onion and garlic and cook for a further 2 minutes, then return all the meat to the pan and pour in the passata. Now add the vinegar, oregano, bay leaf and chopped chilli, and season to taste.

Cover and simmer gently, stirring occasionally, for 1½ hours or until the beef is tender. Taste for seasoning before serving with boiled rice.

cook's note

Chipotles are ripe, dried and smoked chillies. One chipotle will make the stew mildly spicy – use more if you want more heat.

braised ox cheeks with mash

tom parker bowles

Ox cheeks are not always readily available but you can ask your butcher to order them for you. They need to be cooked for a long time to ensure they are tender.

serves 4

preparation time: 20–50 minutes, depending on whether you prepare the ox cheek yourself

cooking time: 2 hours 15 minutes

2 ox cheeks, about 300–400g (10–14oz) each prepared weight (ask your butcher to prepare these by removing the skin and fat)

Plain flour, for dusting

1 tbsp vegetable oil

200ml (7fl oz) stout, London Porter if possible

2 celery sticks, trimmed and cut into chunky matchstick lengths

1 large leek, trimmed, halved and sliced

2 large carrots, peeled and roughly chopped

1 litre (1³/4 pints) chicken stock

A large glug of Worcestershire sauce

Buttery mashed potatoes, to serve

Chop the ox cheeks into 4–6 pieces then dust them with flour. Heat the vegetable oil in a frying pan and brown the meat.

Transfer the meat to a large saucepan or casserole dish. Deglaze the frying pan with a splash of the beer and pour it over the meat. Add the celery, leek and carrots to the pan and cover with the stock. Pour in the Worcestershire sauce and the rest of the beer. Bring to the boil, then reduce the heat and simmer gently for about 1¹/2 hours or until the meat is tender.

Remove the meat from the pan and boil the remaining liquid until it has thickened slightly, about 20 minutes. Return the ox cheeks to the gravy to warm them through, then serve with mashed potato in a bowl with the gravy.

side
dishes

kasha

rose prince

The Russian word 'kasha' means porridge, but in English it generally refers to buckwheat. This salad is great served with leftover roast chicken and soft-boiled eggs.

serves 4

preparation time: 20 minutes
cooking time: 25 minutes

200g (7oz) buckwheat groats,
   (see cook's note)
2 garlic cloves, peeled and
   crushed
A pinch of dried thyme
About 300g (10oz) purple
   sprouting broccoli, trimmed
Juice of 1 lemon
6 tbsp extra virgin olive oil
A small bunch of fresh dill,
   coarsely chopped
Salt and freshly ground black
   pepper

to serve:
Cold cooked chicken
Soft-boiled eggs, peeled

Rinse the buckwheat well in a sieve under cold running water, then place in a saucepan with the garlic and thyme. Cover with cold water and bring to the boil, then reduce the heat to a simmer and cook gently for 15–20 minutes or until tender.

Drain the buckwheat and rinse quickly in cold water to remove any foamy starch. Leave to drain for a few minutes (the groats should not be wet). If necessary, drain and dry on kitchen paper.

Blanch the broccoli in a pan of boiling salted water for 1–2 minutes, then drain and plunge into a bowl of cold water. Drain again thoroughly, slice into long strips and place in a salad bowl. Pour over the lemon juice and olive oil.

Add the drained buckwheat and dill and season to taste. Toss quickly to combine. Serve with cold chicken and soft-boiled eggs.

cook's note

Kasha can be made from any cereal, especially buckwheat, wheat, oats and rye. For salads like this, be sure to buy buckwheat groats as these retain their shape when cooked. Packets labelled simply 'roasted buckwheat' are not suitable as the grains break down during cooking and become mushy like porridge.

spicy slaw

bill granger

This slaw is the perfect accompaniment to barbecue and picnic foods, such as the Lemongrass and Lime Chicken Burgers on p.85

serves 4

preparation time: 15 minutes, plus marinating

for the slaw:
2 tbsp caster sugar
2 tbsp rice or white wine vinegar
2 carrots, peeled and cut into thin matchsticks
75g (3oz) white cabbage, shredded
75g (3oz) red cabbage, shredded
4 celery sticks, trimmed and cut into thin matchsticks
1 red onion, peeled and thinly sliced
A large handful of fresh mint leaves, roughly chopped, plus extra to serve
A large handful of fresh coriander leaves, roughly chopped, plus extra to serve

for the sweet chilli dressing:
2 fresh long red chillies
1 tbsp rice or white wine vinegar
1 tbsp caster sugar
1 1/2 tbsp lime juice
2 tbsp fish sauce

To make the slaw, mix the sugar and vinegar together in a bowl, then add the carrots and stir to mix. Cover and leave to marinate for 20 minutes, stirring occasionally.

For the dressing, deseed and finely chop the chillies then mix together with the remaining dressing ingredients in a separate large bowl. Stir until the sugar has dissolved. Add the cabbages, celery, onion and herbs and mix well. Drain the carrots, add to the slaw and toss together.

stir-fried brussels sprouts with bacon, carrot, parsnip and chestnuts

paul merrett

A great way to convince even the most passionate sprout hater that this often maligned vegetable can taste truly delicious.

serves 4

preparation time: 10 minutes
cooking time: 15 minutes

30 Brussels sprouts
Salt and freshly ground black
   pepper
2 tbsp duck or goose fat
6 rashers streaky bacon,
   chunkily chopped
1 large parsnip, peeled and cut
   into 1cm (1/2in) dice
1 large carrot, peeled and cut
   into matchsticks
1 garlic clove, peeled and
   roughly chopped
8 roasted chestnuts (vacuum
   packed are good)

Bring a large saucepan of water to the boil while you remove the outside leaves from the sprouts. Keep a little stalk intact or the sprouts will fall apart during cooking. Get ready a large bowl of iced water.

Add salt to the boiling water and then the sprouts and boil for 4–5 minutes or until the sprouts are just tender when pierced with a fork. Drain and plunge the sprouts into the iced water to stop them cooking. Leave until cool then drain again. Leave small sprouts whole and cut medium or large sprouts into halves or quarters.

Put the fat into a wok or deep, large frying pan and place over a medium–high heat. When the fat is hot, add the bacon and cook for 2 minutes, then add the parsnip. Cook for 5–7 minutes or until the parsnip turns golden brown, then stir in the carrot and garlic and cook for a further 5 minutes until the vegetables are tender.

Keep the chestnuts whole or break them up a little, then add to the pan along with the sprouts. Toss until heated through, add seasoning to taste and serve straight away.

simple side salad

jun tanaka

The perfect accompaniment to fish or meat, or serve as a light lunch with fresh bread.

serves 4   vegetarian

preparation time: 15 minutes

2 tbsp red wine vinegar
8 tbsp olive oil
Salt and freshly ground pepper
2 garlic cloves, peeled and sliced
3 handfuls of small mixed variety
    tomatoes, sliced in half
2–3 handfuls of radishes, sliced
Fresh herbs of your choice

Whisk the vinegar and olive oil together in a bowl, then season to taste. Stir in the garlic, add the sliced tomatoes and leave for 1–2 minutes for the dressing to infuse the tomatoes.

Arrange the tomatoes on a serving plate and drizzle over the dressing. Scatter with the sliced radishes and lots of fresh herbs.

potato chips

jun tanaka

For the ultimate chip, steam and chill before deep-frying twice. Perfect to dip in a good-quality tomato ketchup.

serves 4   vegetarian

preparation time: 5 minutes
cooking time: 20 minutes, plus
    cooling

4 large Maris Piper potatoes,
    peeled
Enough vegetable oil for
    deep-frying
Tomato ketchup, to serve
    (optional)

Cut the potatoes into 2cm (3/4in) wide x 6cm (1 1/2in) long chips. Steam in a steaming basket (or in an electric combi-steamer), for 8–10 minutes or until cooked through but holding their form and you can crush them lightly with your fingers. Lay the chips on a tray lined with kitchen paper and chill for about 20 minutes.

Pour the vegetable oil into a deep fryer and heat to 150°C (300°F). Deep-fry the chips, in batches if necessary, for 3 minutes or until lightly coloured. Lift out and drain on kitchen paper. Increase the oil temperature to 180°C (350°F) and deep-fry the chips again for 1 minute or until golden brown. Lift out, drain again and serve immediately with ketchup, if desired.

jersey royal potato salad

matt tebbutt

Spring sees the start of the prized Jersey Royal potato season. The heat from the potato will warm through the trout, but as it is added raw make sure it is fresh.

serves 4

preparation time: 15 minutes
cooking time: 15 minutes

500g (1lb 2oz) Jersey Royal
    new potatoes
1/2 cucumber, diced
3 anchovy fillets, finely chopped
1 tsp baby capers
1 tsp cornichons, chopped
1 heaped tsp chopped fresh
    chervil
1 heaped tsp chopped fresh
    chives
1 heaped tsp chopped fresh
    tarragon leaves
2 tbsp crème fraîche
1 tbsp olive oil, plus extra for
    drizzling
Salt and freshly ground black
    pepper
400g (14oz) raw sea trout,
    diced
A bunch of watercress, thick
    stalks removed
Juice of 1/2 lemon

Cook the potatoes in a pan of boiling water for about 15 minutes. Drain, then dice the potatoes. While the potatoes are still warm, stir in the cucumber, anchovies, capers, cornichons, herbs, crème fraîche and the tablespoon of olive oil. Season.

Stir in the diced fish. Season again to taste if necessary, also adding a little more olive oil to moisten, if needed. Serve at room temperature with a helping of watercress dressed lightly with olive oil and the lemon juice.

swiss chard gratin

matthew fort

It is usual to remove the leaves from the stalks of chard before cooking as the different textures of the plant require different cooking times.

serves 4

preparation time: 25 minutes
cooking time: 50 minutes

500g (1lb 2oz) Swiss chard,
    preferably with thick stems
Freshly ground black pepper
150g (5oz) back bacon rashers
125g (4½oz) Gruyère cheese,
    finely grated
250g (9oz) ready-made
    shortcrust pastry
60g (2½oz) Parmesan cheese,
    coarsely grated
Olive oil, for drizzling

23cm (9in) loose-bottomed
    fluted flan tin

Strip the chard leaves from their stalks. Bring a large saucepan of water to the boil and plunge the chard leaves into it. Count to 10, then remove the leaves with a slotted spoon and plunge briefly into a bowl of iced water. Drain and squeeze dry, then chop roughly and place in a bowl.

Chop the chard stalks roughly and blanch in the same pan of boiling water for 3 minutes. Drain thoroughly and tip into the bowl with the leaves. Season with pepper.

Cut the bacon into thin strips and fry gently for 5–10 minutes. Remove and mix into the chard stalks and leaves along with the grated Gruyère.

Place a baking sheet in the oven and preheat the oven to 200°C (400°F), Gas mark 6.

Roll out the pastry on a floured work surface and use to line the flan tin. Line the pastry with foil or greaseproof paper and fill with baking beans. Place the tin on the hot baking sheet and bake blind for 10 minutes, then lift out the foil or paper and beans and return the pastry-lined tin to the oven for a further 5 minutes.

Remove from the oven and fill with the chard, bacon and Gruyère mixture. Sprinkle the grated Parmesan on top and drizzle over a little olive oil. Bake for 20–25 minutes or until the pastry is fully cooked and the top is nicely browned.

up the market
matthew fort

'What breed are the pigs?' I asked, looking at the neat packages of bacon, sausages, pancetta, salamis, cured meats, chorizo, black pudding and other piggy delights.

'Saddleback and Gloucester Old Spot,' said the man sporting a goatee beard and a pork pie hat.

'Organic?' I asked.

'No,' he said, 'but they're reared out doors.'

'Where did you learn to do charcuterie like this?' I asked.

'France, Italy, Germany, Britain,' said the man with the goatee and the pork pie hat.

'I'll have some pork sausages. Plain if you don't mind. And some black pudding. And some of the pancetta. In the piece.'

Can you imagine a conversation like that in a supermarket? OK, they'll provide chapter and verse and pretty pictures of their suppliers and the animals frolicking hock deep in buttercups, but what about warmth? Smiles. Direct answers to direct questions? I think not. Human contact. That's what lies at the heart of shopping in a market. It turns a duty into a pleasure. You can spend £70, £80 in a supermarket in a trice and yet feel utterly depressed and grumpy. And you can spend the same amount at the market, and wander back with your heart singing and your brain racing with the inspiration of what you're going to do with all the fabulous ingredients you've bought.

Why, here are old carrots glowing like embers, cabbages like green and purple cannonballs edged in frilly outer leaves, creamy white cauliflowers the shape of exotic corals, frothing heaps of curly kale the colour of holly, cheeses you could use as a discus, and ziggurats of bread, all shades of golden brown.

Of course, there's the cheery idea that you're supporting your local producers too, and the community, and none of this food has travelled more than 25 miles to get here, so you're doing your bit for the environment as well. And you're eating seasonally, which probably means that the foods are at their best and cheapest, so you can feel virtuous as well. But better than virtue is joy, pleasure, chat, contact, humour and warmth. And that's what shopping in markets is really about.

balsamic vegetables

arthur potts dawson

Balsamic vinegar reduced on the hob makes a delicious sweet sauce to complement your favourite seasonal vegetables.

serves 4   vegetarian

preparation time: 20 minutes
cooking time: 30 minutes

100ml (3^1/$_2$fl oz) balsamic
    vinegar
2 fresh red chillies
2 long red peppers
2 fennel bulbs, thinly sliced with
    fronds reserved
Olive oil, for drizzling
150g (5oz) red treviso chicory,
    sliced
200–250g (7–9oz) curly kale,
    leaves stripped from stems
1 puntarella heart (optional)
Salt and freshly ground black
    pepper

Bubble the vinegar in a heavy-based saucepan for about 7 minutes or until sticky and reduced by about half. Remove from the heat and keep warm.

Heat a griddle pan until smoking hot. Place the whole chillies and red peppers on the pan and cook over a medium–high heat until lightly charred on all sides, about 10 minutes. Transfer the chillies and peppers to a bowl, cover with cling film and leave to steam until the skins have loosened.

Meanwhile, lightly char the fennel slices on the griddle pan, remove to a plate and drizzle with a little olive oil. Place the fennel fronds in a bowl with the red treviso, drizzle with a little of the reduced vinegar and set aside.

Bring a large pan of salted water to the boil and cook the kale leaves and puntarella (if using) for about 4 minutes or until just tender. Drain.

Scrape or peel the skins off the chillies and peppers, then halve lengthways and scrape away the seeds. Tear the flesh.

To serve, divide the fennel slices among 4 plates, then make separate piles of the chillies and peppers, the treviso salad and the cooked vegetables. Drizzle with the reduced vinegar and some olive oil, and season to taste.

cook's note
If the vinegar reduction is too thick to drizzle at the end, place the pan over a low heat until it becomes liquid again.

best-ever creamy mash

arthur potts dawson

For the best-ever mashed potato use a mouli. If you don't have one use a sieve or a ricer instead. Mash can be made ahead and reheated with more milk and butter just before serving.

serves 4   vegetarian

preparation time: 20 minutes
cooking time: 25 minutes

1kg (2lb 4oz) King Edward
    potatoes, peeled and cut
    into large chunks
Salt and freshly ground pepper
100ml (3 1/2fl oz) milk
50g (2oz) salted butter, diced
50ml (1 3/4fl oz) double cream
Freshly grated nutmeg, to taste

Boil the potatoes in a large pan of lightly salted boiling water for 15–20 minutes or until tender. Meanwhile, pour the milk into a small pan and add the butter, cream, nutmeg and seasoning to taste. Bring just to the boil and remove from the heat. Drain the potatoes in a colander.

Pass the cooked potatoes through a mouli into a bowl, then pour enough of the hot milk mixture through the mill so that all the potato residue goes through it and into the bowl.

Gradually mix the remaining milk mixture into the potatoes – you may not need it all as you don't want the mixture too wet. Beat with a wooden spoon until fluffy and smooth, then reheat if necessary.

minted pea purée

mark hix

This sophisticated version of classic chip-shop mushy peas goes perfectly with battered fish.

serves 6–8   vegetarian

preparation time: 10 minutes
cooking time: 15 minutes

35g (1 1/4oz) butter
1 (large) shallot
400g (14oz) frozen peas
100ml (3 1/2fl oz) vegetable stock
6–8 fresh mint leaves
Salt and freshly ground pepper

Heat 25g (1oz) of the butter in a medium saucepan. Peel and chop the shallot and gently fry in the pan until soft, but not browned. Add the peas, vegetable stock and mint. Season. Bring to the boil, then reduce the heat and simmer for 10–12 minutes.

Tip the contents of the pan into a blender or food processor and blend to a coarse purée, adding the rest of the butter. Taste and check for seasoning, adding salt and pepper as required.

braised red cabbage

matt tebbutt

This wintry side dish is great with venison or a Sunday roast.

serves 4   vegetarian

preparation time: 15 minutes
cooking time: 1¼–1½ hours

2 white onions, peeled and
    thinly sliced
50g (2oz) butter
3 tbsp extra virgin olive oil
Salt and freshly ground pepper
2 large Bramley apples, peeled,
    cored and sliced
2 fresh rosemary sprigs
1 red cabbage, about 750g/1lb
    10oz, cored and thinly sliced
90g (3½oz) light soft brown
    sugar
50ml (1¾fl oz) balsamic vinegar

In a large saucepan, sweat the onions in the butter and olive oil. At this point season but don't allow to colour. Throw in the apples and rosemary and stir to break the apples down. Now add the cabbage. This will almost certainly fill the whole pan but don't panic, after a few minutes of vigorous stirring the cabbage will start to shrink.

Cover the pan with a heavy lid to prevent the steam from escaping and reduce the heat to low. The cabbage will now cook for about 45 minutes–1 hour to become tender. Don't let the cabbage stick and burn, so check occasionally and give it a stir, adding a splash of water if it's getting too dry.

When the cabbage is tender, turn the heat up to high and stir in the sugar. Let it caramelise for a few minutes, then add the vinegar and reduce for about 5 minutes or until it has all gone, stirring frequently. Taste for seasoning and serve.

yorkshire pudding

james martin

For the ultimate accompaniment to a Sunday roast, always make the batter by hand and don't be tempted to open the oven door halfway through to take a peek!

makes 16

preparation time: 10 minutes, plus chilling
cooking time: 45 minutes

225g (8oz) plain flour
Salt and freshly ground black pepper
8 eggs
600ml (1 pint) milk
55g (2oz) dripping

12-hole muffin tin

Place the flour and a little salt and pepper into a large bowl, add the eggs, mixing them in with a whisk by hand, then gradually pour in the milk, mixing slowly to prevent lumps forming. Cover with cling film and chill in the fridge overnight.

Preheat the oven to 220°C (425°F), Gas mark 7.

Place a little of the dripping in 10 of the holes of the muffin tin, leaving the middle 2 holes empty (to give room for the puddings to rise). Place the tin in the oven for about 10 minutes until the dripping is smoking hot.

Stir the batter. Carefully remove the tin from the oven as the fat is very hot and quickly fill the moulds with the batter using a ladle or a jug. Return the tin to the oven (the puddings rise a lot, so put them on the middle shelf or lower) and cook for 20–25 minutes.

Turn the oven temperature down to 190°C (375°F), Gas mark 5 and cook for a further 10 minutes to set the bottom of the puddings. Don't open the oven door until the end of cooking or the puddings will deflate. Serve at once. Repeat with the rest of the batter (there is enough for about 6 more puddings).

kale pilaf

rachel allen

Kale is in season during the winter months and this pilaf is the perfect accompaniment to casseroles and stews, such as the slow-cooked beef stroganoff on page 124.

serves 4

preparation time: 10 minutes
cooking time: 25 minutes

50g (2oz) butter
1 small onion, peeled and
  chopped
300g (10oz) basmati rice
750ml (1¼ pints) chicken or
  vegetable stock
Salt and freshly ground black
  pepper
200–225g (7–8oz) curly kale,
  chopped
2 tbsp water

Melt half of the butter in a large saucepan, add the onion, cover and cook over a low heat for about 10 minutes until the onion is soft.

Increase the heat, add the rice and stir for about 2 minutes. Pour in the stock, add some salt and pepper, and bring to the boil. Now turn the heat down as low as possible, and cover the pan again. Simmer for about 10 minutes, or until the rice is just cooked and all the liquid absorbed. Remove from the heat and leave the rice to stand, covered, while you cook the kale.

Melt the remaining butter in a large saucepan, add the kale and water, and cook over a medium heat for 3–4 minutes or until the kale is just wilted.

To serve, fold the kale through the rice and season to taste.

desserts
& cakes

pear and apple crumble with honey mascarpone

aaron craze

For an alternative quick crumble a handful of muesli is a good substitute for more traditional toppings and you won't even need an oven!

serves 4

preparation time: 20 minutes
cooking time: about 25 minutes

2 large handfuls of good-quality
   muesli (about 100g/3 1/2oz)
75g (3oz) plain flour
100g (3 1/2oz) butter, diced
9 tbsp soft light brown sugar
2 Bramley apples, peeled,
   cored and cut into eighths
2 firm but ripe Williams pears,
   peeled, cored and cut into
   eighths
Olive oil, for frying
2 bay leaves
1 cinnamon stick
125ml (4fl oz) Vin Santo (Italian
   sweet white wine)

for the honey mascarpone:
125g (4 1/2oz) mascarpone
2 tbsp clear honey

Mix the muesli and flour together in a bowl, add the butter and rub it in with your fingertips until evenly mixed, then stir in 4 tablespoons of the sugar. Place a large frying pan over a medium heat, tip in the crumble mix and spread out in a single layer. Cook for about 10 minutes until toasted and golden, shaking the pan and turning the mix over occasionally to ensure even colouring. Leave in a warm place.

Place the apples and pears in another large frying pan, add a splash of olive oil and place the pan over a medium heat. Sprinkle the remaining sugar evenly over the fruit and cook for a few minutes until the sugar starts to caramelise and the apples and pears are golden underneath. Add the bay leaves and cinnamon, then the wine. Once the alcohol has evaporated, add a splash of water to create a sauce and continue to cook until the sauce thickens and the fruit feels tender when gently pierced. This should take about 10 minutes, but it will depend on the ripeness of the pears and you may need to add more water.

Meanwhile, stir the mascarpone vigorously in a small bowl to make it smooth, then add the honey and stir until combined.

To serve, divide the fruit mixture evenly among 4 bowls, discarding the bay leaves and cinnamon, and sprinkle the crumble mixture on top. Serve the honey mascarpone on the side.

caramelised peaches with mascarpone

angela hartnett

This dish of Italian-style peaches makes an impressive dinner party dessert and takes just 15 minutes to make. Nectarines and apricots would also work well with these flavours.

serves 4

preparation time: 10 minutes
cooking time: 20 minutes

250g (9oz) mascarpone
1–2 tbsp clear honey, to taste
100g (3½oz) caster sugar
50g (2oz) butter, diced
4 ripe but firm peaches, cut in half, stoned and cut into quarters
100ml (3½oz) Disaronno (amaretto) liqueur

Preheat the oven to 200°C (400°F), Gas mark 6.

Stir the mascarpone vigorously in a small bowl to make it smooth, add honey to taste and stir until evenly combined. Set aside.

Heat a heavy-based ovenproof frying pan over a medium heat until hot. Sprinkle the sugar in an even layer over the base of the pan and heat until it forms a light caramel, about 5 minutes. Turn off the heat and add the butter, swirling the caramel around in the pan until all the butter has melted.

Add the peaches to the pan and turn them to coat in the caramel, then return the pan to a low heat and cook gently for about 10 minutes until the peaches just start to catch in the pan. Deglaze the pan with the liqueur.

Transfer the pan to the oven and bake for about 4 minutes to finish off. Serve the peaches hot with the juices from the pan, and the mascarpone.

condensed milk ice cream with welsh shortbread and raspberry salad

bryn williams

A delicious pudding from one of Wales' finest chefs using a store-cupboard favourite – condensed milk.

serves 4

preparation time: 45 minutes, plus chilling and freezing
cooking time: 45 minutes

for the ice cream:
135g (4³/₄oz) condensed milk
1 litre (1³/₄ pints) milk
25g (1oz) caster sugar

for the shortbread:
100g (3¹/₂oz) slightly salted butter
45g (1¹/₂oz) icing sugar, sifted
125g (4¹/₂oz) plain flour, sifted
A pinch of salt

for the raspberry salad:
350g (12oz) fresh raspberries
2 tbsp caster sugar
Juice of 1 lime
A handful of shelled unsalted pistachio nuts, chopped

For the ice cream, place the condensed milk in a large bowl and set aside. In a heavy-based saucepan, slowly bring the 1 litre (1³/₄ pints) milk and the sugar to the boil, stirring frequently. Continue boiling until reduced by half, stirring frequently to prevent a skin forming, then remove from the heat and skim off any skin from the top with a spoon. Pass the milk through a sieve into the condensed milk in the bowl and mix together. Cover, place in the fridge and leave until the mixture is chilled, about 2 hours.

Transfer the mixture to an ice-cream machine and churn for about 20 minutes or according to the manufacturer's instructions. When churned, transfer the ice cream to a plastic container, seal with a lid and freeze for 2–4 hours to firm up (it will keep in the freezer for up to 2 weeks).

For the shortbread, beat the butter and icing sugar together in a bowl, then lightly mix in the flour and salt to make a dough. Turn the dough out on to a floured surface and roll into a cylinder about 6cm (2¹/₂in) in diameter. Wrap in cling film and chill for at least 2 hours until firm.

Preheat the oven to 200°C (400°F), Gas mark 6.

Cut the chilled dough into 12–14 slices and place on a large baking sheet, spacing them well apart to allow for spreading. Bake for 10–12 minutes or until golden around the edges. Leave on the sheet for 1–2 minutes, then lift onto a wire rack with a palette knife and leave to cool.

For the salad, purée 100g (3$^{1}/_{2}$oz) of the raspberries in a blender or food processor with the sugar and lime juice. Mix the remaining raspberries with the purée in a serving bowl and scatter the pistachios on top.

To serve, transfer the ice cream to the fridge for about 30 minutes to soften before scooping. Serve with a dollop of raspberry salad and the shortbread.

tiramisu cake with mascarpone and vanilla cream

matt tebbutt

A great alternative to a Victoria sponge, the secret to this cake is to be generous with the syrup, to prevent it drying out.

cuts into 8 slices

preparation time: 20 minutes
cooking time: 40 minutes

175g (6oz) butter
175g (6oz) caster sugar
3 eggs, lightly beaten
175g (6oz) self-raising flour

for the syrup:
90g (3oz) caster sugar
50ml (1³/₄fl oz) water
3 tbsp coffee essence or good-
    quality strong coffee
3 tbsp brandy

**for the mascarpone and vanilla
    cream:**
250g (9oz) mascarpone
125g (4¹/₂oz) crème fraîche
1 vanilla pod, split lengthways
    and seeds scraped out
2 tbsp icing sugar, sifted

20cm (8in) diameter and
    6.5–7cm (3in) deep
    spring-form/loose-bottomed
    cake tin

Preheat the oven to 180°C (350°F), Gas mark 4. Grease and base-line the cake tin.

Cream the butter and sugar together in a bowl until pale and fluffy. Gradually add the eggs, beating constantly, then fold in the flour. Spoon the mixture into the cake tin and bake for 40 minutes or until a skewer inserted into the centre comes out clean. Cool for a while in the tin, about 15 minutes.

Meanwhile, make the syrup. Heat the sugar in a saucepan with the water, coffee and brandy until the sugar has dissolved.

Remove the cake from the tin and place on a serving plate. While the cake is still warm, prick all over the top with a skewer or fork and slowly spoon the syrup over it, waiting until it is absorbed before adding more.

For the mascarpone and vanilla cream, stir the mascarpone vigorously in a small bowl to make it smooth, then beat in the crème fraîche, vanilla seeds and icing sugar. Serve the cake warm with the mascarpone and vanilla cream.

cook's note
If you like, you can make double the quantity of syrup and serve half in a jug for pouring at the table.

clementine and orange blossom clafoutis

jun tanaka

This makes a delicious alternative Christmas dessert using seasonal clementines. You could, however, use any fruit that happens to be in season.

serves 6

preparation time: 20 minutes
cooking time: 35 minutes

120g (4½oz) caster sugar, plus extra for dusting
8 clementines, peeled and segmented
150ml (5fl oz) double cream
150ml (5fl oz) whole milk
5 eggs
4 tsp orange-flower (blossom) water
25g (1oz) plain flour

to serve:
Icing sugar, for dusting
Natural yogurt, soured cream or crème fraîche

1.3–1.4 litre (2¼–2½ pint) shallow ovenproof dish

Preheat the oven to 190°C (375°F), Gas mark 5. Grease the inside of the ovenproof dish, then dust with a little caster sugar. Arrange the clementines on the base.

To make the batter, pour the cream and milk into a medium saucepan and bring just to the boil. Remove from the heat. Break 2 whole eggs and the yolks of 3 into a mixing bowl. Whisk the eggs and sugar together until just well mixed, then whisk in the orange-flower water and flour. Finally, slowly whisk in the hot cream and milk.

Pour the batter mix over the clementines in the dish and bake for 30–35 minutes until firm, slightly puffy on top and cooked through. Remove from the oven, dust with icing sugar and serve with yogurt, soured cream or crème fraîche.

individual pear tartes tatins

mark sargeant

This is a delicious twist on this classic French tart using pears instead of apples.

serves 4

preparation time: 20 minutes
cooking time: 30 minutes

2 firm pears
4 star anise
1 vanilla pod, cut into 4 pieces
1 x 500g (1lb 2oz) packet
  ready-made puff pastry
Icing sugar, for dusting

for the caramel:
100g (3½oz) caster sugar
100g (3½oz) unsalted butter,
  cubed
A splash of dark rum
Vanilla ice cream, to serve

Preheat the oven to 220°C (425°F), Gas mark 7.

Peel the pears, halve them lengthways and scoop out the cores using a melon baller to create a small round hole. Press a star anise into each hole. Use a small, sharp knife to cut out the stalks and insert a piece of vanilla pod into each incision to form a 'stalk'.

Roll out the pastry on a lightly floured surface to a large sheet about 3mm (1/8in) thick, then cut the dough into 4 even-sized pieces. Mould each piece of pastry around the peeled outer side of each pear to form a 'blanket', leaving the cut-side of the pear exposed. Trim away any excess pastry and place the pears in the fridge, cut-side down on a board or plate to chill while you make the caramel.

Scatter the sugar for the caramel into a large, heavy-based, ovenproof frying pan and cook over a medium heat for about 5 minutes, without stirring, until the sugar has dissolved and turned a golden caramel colour. To prevent the mixture spitting, reduce the heat and add the butter, swirling the pan so the butter dissolves into the caramel. Carefully pour in the rum and swirl around to loosen the caramel.

Remove the pears from the fridge and place them cut-side down on top of the caramel in the pan. Generously dust the pastry with icing sugar then transfer the pan to the oven and bake for 15–20 minutes or until the pastry is crisp and golden. Leave to stand for 1–2 minutes, then carefully slide a palette knife under each pear and flip it over onto a warm serving plate, pastry-side down. Drizzle over the pan juices and serve with vanilla ice cream.

spiced crème brûlée with coffee syrup

tom aikens

The traditional crème brûlée receives a spicy makeover using liquorice and ginger. Cinnamon, star anise and juniper berries are delicious as well.

serves 4

preparation time: 25 minutes, plus infusing and chilling

cooking time: 1 hour, plus cooling

375ml (13fl oz) double cream
125ml (4fl oz) whole milk
2 cinnamon sticks
10 star anise
1/2 tsp cloves
1cm (1/2in) piece fresh root ginger, peeled and sliced
20g (3/4oz) liquorice root, sliced or broken (available in health food shops)
2 vanilla pods, split lengthways, seeds scraped out
75g (3oz) palm sugar, finely grated (or buy as granulated palm sugar)
5 egg yolks

for the coffee syrup:
2 tbsp coffee granules
200ml (7fl oz) water
125g (4 1/2oz) caster sugar
Lemon juice, to taste

Four 150ml (5fl oz) ramekin dishes

Pour the cream and milk into a medium saucepan and add the spices, liquorice and vanilla pods (reserving the seeds). Heat until warm, then leave to cool for 15–20 minutes.

Meanwhile, for the coffee syrup, place the coffee granules in a medium saucepan, add the water and sugar and bring slowly to the boil to dissolve the sugar. Boil to reduce by at least two-thirds until it becomes a thick syrup, about 15 minutes. Pass through a sieve and add enough lemon juice to take the edge off the sweetness. Leave to cool, then set aside until ready to serve.

Whisk the palm sugar, egg yolks and reserved vanilla seeds together in a bowl, then whisk in the cooled cream. Leave this mixture for a day or overnight in the fridge.

The next day, preheat the oven to 150°C (300°F), Gas mark 2.

Mix the custard mixture again and pass through a sieve to remove the spices. Place the ramekins in a deep roasting tin and divide the custard mixture among them. Pour enough boiling water around the outside of the ramekins to come three-quarters of the way up the sides of the dishes and bake for 40–45 minutes or until firm, but slightly wobbly in the middle. Cool briefly, then chill for at least 30 minutes or overnight.

To serve, drizzle a little of the coffee syrup on top of each custard.

spiced pears with chocolate mousse

tristan welch

A reinvention of the classic school-dinner pudding of pears with chocolate sauce. The use of spices and the luxurious chocolate mousse makes this an impressive restaurant-style dessert.

serves 4

preparation time: 25 minutes
cooking time: 20 minutes

4 ripe Conference pears
75g (3oz) butter
1½ cinnamon sticks, broken into pieces
7 cloves
2 star anise

for the chocolate mousse:
75ml (2½fl oz) water
½ small cinnamon stick
2 whole cloves
1 star anise
100g (3½oz) plain dark chocolate (at least 70% cocoa solids), broken into small pieces

For the pears, peel them and cut a thin slice off the bottom of each so they stand upright. Melt the butter in a heavy-based frying pan over a medium–high heat and add the spices. As soon as the butter starts to foam, add the pears and turn them to coat in the butter. Cook for 10–15 minutes, turning the pears and spooning over the spiced butter every few minutes (take care the butter doesn't burn), until they are just tender but still holding their shape. When the pears are cooked, remove from the heat and set aside.

While the pears are cooking make the chocolate mousse. Pour the water into a small saucepan and add the spices. Bring to a simmer then remove from the heat. Place the chocolate pieces in a medium heatproof bowl and sit a sieve over the bowl. Fill another larger bowl with ice cubes. Strain the spice-infused hot water through the sieve onto the chocolate pieces, then whisk until the chocolate melts and combines with the water to form a smooth consistency (discard the spices). Sit the bowl containing the chocolate inside the ice-filled bowl, stirring the mixture constantly until it just starts to thicken and set, but not become too firm. Remove from the ice and shape the mixture into quenelles using a dessertspoon.

Return the pears to the heat, allowing them and the juices to warm through, then add a splash of water and simmer for 1 minute to create a glaze.

To serve, stand the pears upright on 4 serving plates, drizzle over the spiced butter glaze and place a spoonful of chocolate mousse alongside.

amanda's brother's cheesecake

amanda lamb

This baked cheesecake using cream cheese gives an authentic taste of New York. Make sure the cheese, cream and eggs are whipped until smooth to avoid a lumpy texture. You could also decorate the top with your favourite fruit.

cuts into 8 slices

preparation time: 15 minutes, plus chilling
cooking time: 55 minutes

200g (7oz) digestive biscuits
50g (2oz) butter, diced
740g (1lb 10oz) full-fat soft cheese, such as Philadelphia
225g (8oz) golden caster sugar
3 tbsp cornflour
Seeds of 2 vanilla pods
A few drops of vanilla extract
2 eggs, beaten
240ml (8$\frac{1}{2}$fl oz) double cream

23–24cm (9–9$\frac{1}{2}$in) diameter and 6.6–7cm (2$\frac{3}{4}$in) deep spring-form/loose-bottomed cake tin

Preheat the oven to 180°C (350°F), Gas mark 4. Grease and base-line the cake tin.

Break the biscuits into a blender or processor and process to a crumb consistency. Melt the butter in a small pan and mix with the biscuit crumbs in a bowl. Tip the mixture into the cake tin and press firmly over the paper on the base to make an even layer. Chill for about 30 minutes or until set.

Using an electric mixer on its slowest setting, combine the cheese, sugar, cornflour, vanilla seeds and extract until smooth and thick. Add the eggs and cream and continue to mix until very thick. Spoon into the tin to make a smooth, even layer over the biscuit base.

Bake for 45 minutes or until set in the centre, then increase the oven temperature to 200°C (400°F), Gas mark 6 for 10 minutes to brown the top. Remove from the oven and leave until cold, then chill in the fridge until ready to serve.

lemon-drenched yogurt cake

diana henry

This mouth-watering yet simple cake is perfect for those who are scared of baking. Use a springform tin so that the cake can be plated without sticking once it's cool. Springform tins can be bought at any good kitchen shop.

serves 12

preparation time: 25 minutes
cooking time: 50 minutes, plus
   cooling

for the syrup:
175g (6oz) caster sugar
Juice of 1¹/₂ lemons (about
   5 tbsp)
275ml (9¹/₂fl oz) water

for the cake:
200g (7oz) self-raising flour
110g (4oz) ground almonds
150g (5oz) caster sugar
A good pinch of salt
1 tsp baking powder
2 eggs, beaten
250g (9oz) plain Greek yogurt
150ml (5fl oz) sunflower oil

to serve:
Icing sugar
Fresh summer berries
Crème fraîche or Greek yogurt

20cm (8in) diameter spring-form
   cake tin

Preheat the oven to 180°C (350°F), Gas mark 4. Grease and base-line the cake tin.

For the syrup, place the sugar and lemon juice in a medium, heavy-based saucepan then pour in the water. Heat gently, stirring to help the sugar dissolve. Once dissolved, bring the mixture to the boil and boil for 7 minutes. Leave to cool.

For the cake, sift the flour into a large bowl. Add the almonds, sugar, salt and baking powder, stir to mix, then make a well in the centre. Place the eggs, yogurt and oil into the well and stir with a wooden spoon, gradually incorporating the wet ingredients into the dry ones.

Spoon the mixture into the tin, level the top and bake for 40–45 minutes or until a skewer inserted into the middle of the cake comes out clean. Leave the cake to cool in the tin for 10 minutes, then turn it out, remove the lining paper and place the cake on a plate that has a slight dip in it to catch the syrup. While the cake is still warm, pierce holes all over the top with a skewer and slowly spoon the syrup over, letting it soak in between spoonfuls, until all the syrup is used. Leave to soak in completely.

To serve, dust with icing sugar and serve with berries and crème fraîche.

hazelnut and chocolate croccante

theo randall

The word 'croccante' means crunch, which describes the texture of this dessert perfectly.

serves 4 generously or 6–8 smaller portions

preparation time: 25 minutes
cooking time: 10 minutes

150g (5oz) hazelnuts
100g (3½oz) caster sugar
200g (7oz) dark plain chocolate
    (at least 70% cocoa solids),
    broken into pieces
300ml (10fl oz) double cream,
    lightly whipped
4 tbsp crème fraîche
2 tsp brandy
1 tsp cocoa powder, for dusting

Chilled glasses

Preheat the oven to 190°C (375°F), Gas mark 5.

Place the hazelnuts on a baking sheet and roast for 7–8 minutes until the skins are starting to come off. Oil a piece of greaseproof paper and lay it on another baking sheet.

Tip the sugar into a small, heavy-based frying pan and heat gently until it turns a caramel colour, about 5 minutes. Stir in the nuts and cook for 3–4 minutes over a low heat, then tip out onto the greaseproof paper and leave to set. When set, roughly break up the nuts and place them in a strong plastic bag. Bash with a rolling pin until you get fine crumbs.

Melt the chocolate very gently in a bowl set over a pan of barely simmering water. Don't let the bowl touch the water. Alternatively, microwave it on the defrost setting, checking at 1-minute intervals. Let the chocolate cool slightly but still be runny.

Fold the melted chocolate into the cream and stir in half the crushed hazelnuts. Spoon the mixture into chilled glasses and decorate with the remaining hazelnuts and spoonfuls of crème fraîche. Drizzle a little brandy over each dessert and finish with a dusting of cocoa. Do not refrigerate or the chocolate cream will solidify.

molten chocolate cakes

donna hay

These molten chocolate cakes are foolproof. Rest the cakes for 5 minutes before turning them out onto the plate.

serves 4

preparation time: 20 minutes
cooking time: 30 minutes

160g (5³/₄oz) plain dark
    chocolate, chopped
80g (3¹/₂oz) butter, diced
2 egg whites
55g (2oz) icing sugar
35g (1¹/₄oz) plain flour
90g (3¹/₄oz) ground almonds
4 x 10g (¹/₄oz) squares plain
    dark chocolate

to serve:
Fresh raspberries
Crème fraîche

Four 125ml (4fl oz) ovenproof
    dishes

Preheat the oven to 150°C (300°F), Gas mark 2. Lightly grease the ovenproof dishes.

Melt the chocolate with the butter in a heatproof bowl set over a pan of gently simmering water. Don't let the base of the bowl touch the water. Remove the bowl from the pan and set aside.

In a separate bowl, whisk the egg whites until soft peaks form.

Sift the icing sugar and flour into a large bowl. Stir in the almonds and melted chocolate mixture, then fold in the egg whites until evenly combined. Spoon half of the mixture into the dishes, place a chocolate square on top of each one and cover with the remaining mixture. Bake for 20 minutes or until cooked but still gooey in the middle (test by piercing with a skewer). Leave the cakes to stand in their dishes for 5 minutes before turning out and serving with raspberries and crème fraîche.

pecan and banana bran muffins

tana ramsay

These tasty muffins are great for packed lunches or breakfast at the weekend. The addition of bran flakes gives an extra crunch!

makes 12

preparation time: 25 minutes
cooking time: 30 minutes

100g (3¹/₂oz) butter, softened
100g (3¹/₂oz) soft light brown sugar
3 ripe bananas, mashed
60ml (2fl oz) milk
1 tsp vanilla extract
2 eggs, beaten
300g (10oz) plain flour
¹/₂ tsp salt
1 tsp bicarbonate of soda
1 tsp baking powder
200g (7oz) pecans, finely chopped
100g (3¹/₂oz) bran flakes

12-hole muffin tin

Preheat the oven to 190°C (375°F), Gas mark 5. Line the muffin tin with paper muffin cases.

In a very large bowl, cream together the butter and sugar until light and fluffy. Stir in the mashed bananas, milk, vanilla and eggs and combine well. Mix in the flour, salt, bicarbonate of soda and baking powder, then finally fold in the pecans and bran flakes.

Spoon the mixture into the paper muffin cases, dividing it equally among them (the mixture will fill the cases) and bake for 25–30 minutes. Remove and cool the muffins on a wire rack. They will keep for up to 3 days in an airtight tin.

easter orange cake with lemon icing

tana ramsay

This is a light, fresh-tasting alternative to simnel cake at Easter. It's easy to make and kids love getting involved in decorating the top.

serves 12

preparation time: 25 minutes
cooking time: 30 minutes, plus cooling

150g (5oz) unsalted butter, softened to room temperature
150g (5oz) caster sugar
200g (7oz) self-raising flour
3 eggs
Grated zest and juice of 1 large orange

for the icing:
Grated zest and juice of 1 large lemon (about 2 tbsp juice)
175g (6oz) icing sugar, sifted
Easter decorations, such as chicks and mini eggs

20cm (8in) diameter square cake tin

Preheat the oven to 180°C (350°F), Gas mark 4. Grease and base-line the cake tin.

In a large mixing bowl, beat together the butter, caster sugar, flour and eggs until light and creamy. Stir in the orange zest and juice then spoon the mixture into the cake tin and level the top. Bake for about 30 minutes or until risen and golden and it feels firm to the touch. Leave the cake to cool in the tin for 5–10 minutes, then take it out of the tin, peel off the paper and leave to cool completely on a wire rack.

To make the icing, keep a little lemon zest back for the decoration, then beat the icing sugar, lemon juice and the rest of the zest together to make a smooth, runny icing. Using a palette knife, spread the icing over the top of the cake and let it drizzle down the sides. Leave to set. Scatter over the reserved lemon zest and decorate with Easter decorations.

carrot cake

michael caines

This all-time baking favourite doubles as a dessert when served with an indulgent ice cream.

cuts into about 14 slices

preparation time: 30 minutes
cooking time: 1¼–1½ hours,
  plus cooling

450ml (15fl oz) vegetable oil
400g (14oz) plain flour
570g (1lb 4oz) caster sugar
5 medium eggs
4 tsp ground cinnamon
2 tsp bicarbonate of soda
½ tsp salt
530g (1lb 3oz) peeled and
  grated carrots (675–700g/1lb
  9oz unpeeled)
150g (5oz) walnuts, roughly
  chopped
White chocolate or vanilla ice
  cream, to serve

for the icing:
200g (7oz) full-fat soft cheese,
  preferably Philadelphia
150g (5oz) icing sugar, sifted
100g (3½oz) butter, softened

26cm (10½in) diameter
  and 6.5–7cm (3in) deep
  spring-form/loose-bottomed
  cake tin

Preheat the oven to 180°C (350°F), Gas mark 4. Grease and base-line the cake tin.

Place all the ingredients except the carrots and nuts in a large bowl and beat with an electric mixer for 5 minutes. Add the carrots and nuts and mix through.

Transfer the mixture to the cake tin and bake for 1¼–1½ hours or until a skewer inserted in the centre of the cake comes out clean. Leave the cake to cool for about 20 minutes, then remove from the tin and carefully peel off the lining paper. Place the cake on a wire rack to cool completely.

For the icing, place the cheese, sugar and butter in a bowl and cream together until smooth. Spread over the cold cake using a palette knife, then chill in the fridge until firm. Serve the cake sliced into wedges with small quenelles or scoops of white chocolate or vanilla ice cream.

spanish lemon ice

rachel allen

This deliciously fragrant ice cream is the perfect cooling dessert on a hot summer's day.

serves 6

preparation time: 10 minutes
freezing time: overnight

1 egg, separated
250ml milk
140g caster sugar
Grated zest and juice of
    1 lemon

Whisk the egg yolk with the milk. Add the sugar and the grated zest and juice of the lemon.

In a separate bowl, whisk the egg whites until stiff then fold into the lemon mixture.

Freeze in a sorbetière. Alternatively, pour into a shallow container and half freeze. Remove and whisk or break it up in a food processor, then put it back into the freezer. This prevents ice crystals forming.

Leave in the freezer overnight to firm before serving.

soft chocolate cake with crema di mascarpone

theo randall

This beautiful flourless chocolate cake works best with 66 per cent chocolate.

serves 14

preparation time: 40 minutes
cooking time: 45 minutes

400g (14oz) Valhrona chocolate (at least 70% cocoa solids), or good-quality plain dark chocolate, broken or chopped into small pieces
6 eggs
150g (5oz) caster sugar
300ml (10fl oz) double cream

for the crema di mascarpone:
150ml (5fl oz) double cream
200g (7oz) mascarpone
1/2 vanilla pod, split lengthways and seeds scraped out
50g (2oz) icing sugar, sifted
25ml (1fl oz) Marsala

20cm (8in) deep round cake tin (not spring-form/loose-bottomed)

Preheat the oven to 170°C (325°F), Gas mark 3. Grease and line the base and sides of the cake tin with parchment paper, then lightly flour the base. Nearly half-fill with water a large, deep ovenproof container for the bain-marie and place in the oven.

Melt the chocolate in a bowl over a pan of simmering water. Do not let the base of the bowl touch the water. When melted, remove from the heat, but don't let the chocolate get too cool.

Separate the eggs, putting the yolks into a medium bowl and the whites into a large one. Whisk the yolks with 100g (3^1/2oz) of the caster sugar until the mixture is pale in colour and makes a ribbon trail as it falls when the beaters are lifted up.

In another bowl, whip 150ml (5fl oz) of the cream until it forms soft peaks. Whisk the egg whites (not too stiffly) then gradually add the remaining 50g (2oz) caster sugar, again to soft peak stage. The mixture should look light and glossy. Finally, mix the melted chocolate into the yolk mixture. Stir in the remaining 150ml (5fl oz) of unwhipped cream, then fold in the whipped cream. Carefully and gradually fold in the egg whites and pour the mixture into the tin. Gently level the top and carefully place the tin in the bain-marie (the water level should be up to the level of the mixture in the tin). Bake for about 45 minutes until the cake is firm on the top with a slight wobble.

Meanwhile, for the crema di mascarpone, gradually mix the cream into the mascarpone, beating until smooth. Stir in the vanilla seeds and enough of the icing sugar and Marsala to taste.

Remove the cake from oven. Leave it in the water to cool, then lift it out of the water. Remove the cake from the tin and peel off the paper. Serve in slices, topped with the crema di mascarpone.

christmas panettone bread and butter pudding

giorgio locatelli

In Northern Italy panettone is traditionally eaten at Christmas. Here it is used to create a delicious twist on the classic British Bread and Butter Pudding.

serves 4

preparation time: 15 minutes, plus resting

cooking time: 20 minutes

400ml (14fl oz) whole milk
50g (2oz) unsalted butter, softened
4–5 slices panettone, cut 1cm (1/2in) thick
2 eggs
25g (1oz) granulated sugar
1 vanilla pod, split lengthways

Four 170ml (6fl oz) ramekin dishes

Preheat the oven to 180°C (350°F), Gas mark 4. Heat the milk to just under simmering point and set aside. Thickly spread the butter on one side of each panettone slice, then cut into chunks. Arrange a few in the bases of the ramekins.

Crack the eggs into a bowl, add the sugar and scrape in the vanilla seeds. Beat with a fork then stir in the warm milk. Pour half the egg and milk mixture over the panettone in the ramekins. Add a second layer of panettone and fill the ramekins with the remaining egg and milk mixture. The bread can poke out of the top slightly.

Place the ramekins in a roasting tin and pour enough boiling water around the outside of the ramekins to come halfway up the sides. Bake for 20 minutes. Remove from the oven, lift the ramekins out of the water and rest for 20 minutes before serving.

summer berries with yogurt and cardamom

rachel allen

Perfect on a summer's day, this is an incredibly quick, easy and light dessert. Orange rind can be used as a delicious alternative to cardamom.

serves 4

preparation time: 15 minutes

300ml (10fl oz) natural yogurt

1 tbsp golden caster sugar, or more to taste

1 tbsp lemon juice, or more to taste

3/4 tsp green cardamom seeds, ground

400g (14oz) summer berries, such as raspberries, sliced strawberries, blueberries

In a bowl, mix the yogurt with the sugar, lemon juice and ground cardamom. Taste and add more sugar or lemon juice, if you like.

Scatter half of the berries into 4 glasses or glass bowls. Spoon half of the yogurt mixture on top, followed by half of the remaining fruit. Finish with the remaining yogurt and fruit. Chill in the fridge until ready to serve.

condiments

pickled shallots

fergus henderson

These spicy shallots are the perfect accompaniment to cold meats and salad.

makes 1kg (2lb 4oz)
vegetarian

preparation time: 10 minutes,
    plus soaking and picking
cooking time: 10 minutes

1kg (2lb 4oz) shallots, peeled
500g/1lb 2oz sea salt
1.5 litres/2³/4 pints water
1 bottle malt vinegar (about
    375ml/13fl oz)
1 bottle white wine vinegar
    (about 375ml/13fl oz)
8 cloves
10 allspice berries
2 cinnamon sticks
8 white peppercorns
10 black peppercorns
4 bay leaves
12 coriander seeds
4 small hot dried chillies

Cover the shallots with brine (made with the salt and water) and leave to soak in a non-metallic container in the fridge for 1 week.

Now you know how much liquid it takes to cover your shallots, combine equal parts of the vinegars to make the same amount. Bring to the boil in a stainless steel pan with the spices and herbs.

Rinse the shallots thoroughly. Add them to the simmering spiced vinegar and cook for 5 minutes. Remove from the heat and bottle in sterilised sealable jars. Keep somewhere cool for a month.

cook's note
The leftover spiced vinegar is very good for dipping cooked whelks in.

sichuan dipping salt

tom parker bowles

Try dipping hard-boiled quails' eggs in this fragrant lemony seasoning for a mouth-watering snack.

**makes 4 tablespoonfuls
(55g/2oz)
vegetarian**

preparation time: 5 minutes
cooking time: 5 minutes

1 tbsp Sichuan peppercorns
3 tbsp sea salt

Heat a small dry wok or heavy-based pan over a low heat, add the peppercorns and stir-fry for about 5 minutes or until the pepper husks are richly fragrant. They will smoke a bit as you cook them. Leave to cool.

Finely grind the peppercorns using a pestle and mortar. Sift the powder to get rid of any stalks or ungrounded husks, then mix with the sea salt. Store in an airtight container.

spanish marinated olives

thomasina miers

These olives are the perfect accompaniment to a glass of dry Spanish sherry. Try experimenting with other herbs, spices and flavourings to serve at a drinks party.

serves 8   vegetarian

preparation time: 5 minutes,
  plus marinating
cooking time: 1 minute

1 tsp cumin seeds
500g (1lb 2oz) green olives, not
  stoned (or more if you want)
Pared zest of 1 unwaxed lemon
  and a squeeze of the juice
2 fresh thyme sprigs
1 large garlic clove, peeled and
  crushed
About 300ml (10fl oz) olive oil

Heat a small heavy-based frying pan, add the cumin seeds and toast briefly until starting to smell fragrant.

Place the olives in a large bowl and add the cumin seeds, lemon zest, thyme and garlic. Pour in enough olive oil so the olives are just covered and a squeeze of lemon juice to flavour, then cover and leave to marinate overnight in a cool place.

If not eating straight away, the olives can be transferred to a sterilised glass jar and kept in the fridge for up to a month.

pickled sun-dried tomatoes

matt tebbutt

Pickled sun-dried tomatoes can be used to add texture and sharpness to pasta sauces or give a great kick to summer salads.

makes 2 x 450g (1lb) jars

preparation time: 10 minutes, plus soaking and maturing
cooking time: 5 minutes

150g (5oz) sun-dried tomatoes
150ml (5fl oz) red wine vinegar
150ml (5fl oz) balsamic vinegar
75g (3oz) light or dark soft brown sugar
1 large fresh rosemary sprig

Place the tomatoes in a bowl, cover with boiling water and leave to soak for 3 hours or until soft and rehydrated.

Meanwhile, place the vinegars, sugar and rosemary in a saucepan, heat gently until the sugar has dissolved, then bring to the boil. Remove from the heat and leave to cool completely.

Drain the tomatoes, divide between 2 sterilised 450g (1lb) jars and pour over the infused vinegars. Seal the jars and leave in the fridge for 1 month before use to allow the flavours to develop.

cook's note
To sterilise jars, immerse clean jars in a pan of water and bring to the boil, then drain and dry thoroughly in a warm oven.

preserved lemons

matt tebbutt

These can be used in all kinds of recipes: chopped and mixed with butter then rubbed on fish, added to roasted vegetables and salads, or used in Moroccan tagines.

makes 1 litre (1³/4 pints) jar

preparation time: 15 minutes, plus preserving

4–6 unwaxed lemons
4–5 tbsp coarse sea salt
1/2 tsp coriander seeds
1 cinnamon stick
2–3 bay leaves
Juice of about 10 lemons

Scrub the lemons clean under cold running water, then cut each lemon in half most of the way through from top to bottom, leaving the bottom attached. Pack salt into the cuts in the lemons and squeeze the fruit closed, then stuff the lemons into a sterilised 1 litre (1³/4 pint) jar with the coriander seeds, cinnamon stick and bay leaves. Pour in enough lemon juice to cover the fruit completely and come up to the top of the jar.

Seal the jar and leave in a cool place to mature for 4–6 weeks or until the lemons are soft.

chilli oil

tom parker bowles

This oil will keep for months in your store cupboard and is a delicious way to flavour any dish.

makes 450ml (15fl oz)
vegetarian

preparation time: 5 minutes,
plus several weeks to infuse
cooking time: 5 minutes

450ml (15fl oz) olive oil (not
extra virgin)
20g (3/4oz) crushed chillies
10g (1/4oz) whole dried chillies

Gently warm the olive oil in a medium saucepan. Add the crushed chillies and whole chillies to the oil and heat for 3–4 minutes.

Using a funnel, decant the oil and chillies into a sterilised glass bottle. Seal and shake well. Store the bottle in a cool, dry and dark place. Once a week give the bottle a shake and after a few weeks the oil will change to a slightly reddish colour. It could take two or three months to achieve the desired hotness. The oil can be kept in the bottle for several months. I usually keep it for 8–10 months.

mark's salad vinaigrette

mark sargeant

For the perfect salad, you need the perfect vinaigrette. This is a kitchen staple you can use time and time again.

makes 400ml (14fl oz)
vegetarian

preparation time: 5 minutes

300ml (10fl oz) olive oil
100ml (3 1/2fl oz) white wine
vinegar
Juice of 1/2 lemon
Salt and freshly ground
black pepper

Blend all the ingredients together in a bowl using a hand blender. Pour through a funnel into a sterilised bottle. Tightly screw a lid on the bottle and shake vigorously. It will keep for up to a month in cool, dry place. Shake again before serving.

peppermint creams

jane fearnley-whittingstall

This simple recipe is perfect for getting kids interested in food – and makes an appetizing sweet treat.

makes about 50 (depending on the size of the cutter)
vegetarian

preparation time: 25 minutes, plus drying

500–550g (1lb 2oz–1lb 3½oz) icing sugar, plus extra for dusting
1 egg white
50ml (1¾fl oz) double cream
Oil of peppermint or peppermint essence

Mix the icing sugar, egg white and cream together, then add the peppermint drop by drop until it tastes right.

Dust a clean, dry surface with icing sugar and roll out the peppermint paste to about 15mm (⅝in) thick. If it's too sticky, keep adding icing sugar until it is the right consistency.

Use a small cutter to stamp out rounds, then leave to dry on parchment paper for 12 hours.

stocking the larder

rachel allen

I love shopping at the market for the freshest ingredients. If I know I've got a well-stocked larder, I can always rustle up a delicious meal with whatever market bounty I've brought home.

When foods are at the height of the season, they are often best cooked very simply. A selection of good-quality oils, vinegars and spices are perfect for this. I stock several kinds of vinegars – red, white, sherry, balsamic, rice and cider vinegar – and a selection of oils – extra virgin olive oil and a good neutral oil such as sunflower oil. I also love seed or nut oils, such as walnut and hazelnut for salad dressings.

I keep jars of whole dried spices like black pepper, cumin seeds, coriander seeds, mustard seeds, cinnamon sticks and nutmeg. Ground spices lose flavour more quickly than whole ones, so I buy smaller quantities of turmeric, ginger and cayenne pepper, and I always have a fine salt for baking and a coarse sea salt for the table and for seasoning.

Soy sauce, fish sauce and sweet chilli sauce keep forever and are a must for Asian cooking. Pastas and a few different varieties of rice, such as basmati and arborio for risottos are essential; as are tinned tomatoes and tins of beans like chickpeas and haricot beans as well as dried beans, such as lentils. Also, I'm never without a supply of eggs, potatoes, onions and garlic.

In the fridge I always have butter, cream, milk, natural yogurt and a variety of cheeses. I also love chorizo, which I like to keep on hand for a bit of spice in sauces, soups and pastas.

I'll often add seeds to baked bread, smoothies and salads. I keep a supply of pumpkin seeds, sesame seeds, golden linseed, flaxseeds, poppy seeds and sunflower seeds. Oats are another essential for porridge, biscuits and even smoothies. I also like to have a variety of nuts such as pecans, hazelnuts and almonds, which I buy in small quantities to keep them fresh.

For baking, I stock plain flour, self-raising flour, wholemeal flour, cornflour, rice flour and baking powder, bicarbonate of soda and cream of tartar as well as different sugars – caster sugar, dark brown sugar and golden syrup – and a good vanilla extract.

I use the freezer to store breadcrumbs and pine nuts. Meat and fish also store perfectly in the freezer, and I like to extend the market season by freezing fresh fruits. If you have a glut of tomatoes or berries in the summer, freeze them for cooking throughout the year.

producers' list

Here are some of *Market Kitchen's* best sources of great ingredients from Borough Market and across the country.

bakery

Flour Power City Bakery Ltd, London
Organic artisan baker.
8 Stoney Street
Borough Market
London SE1 1TL
00 44 (0)20 8691 2288
www.flourpowercity.com

Konditor & Cook, London
Patisserie and confectionery.
10 Stoney Street
Borough Market
London SE1 9AD
00 44 (0)20 7407 5100
www.konditorandcook.com

eggs and dairy

Bower Farm Dairy, Abergavenny
Jersey cream, clotted cream, yogurt and milk from a pedigree Jersey herd.
Grosmont
Abergavenny
Monmouthshire
NP7 8HS
00 44 (0)1981 240219
Email: collinson@bowerfarm.freeserve.co.uk

Neal's Yard Dairy, London
Cheeses – specialises in farm cheese from the British Isles.
6 Park Street
London SE1 9AB
00 44 (0)20 7367 0799
www.nealsyarddairy.co.uk

Paxton & Whitfield, London
Cheeses.
93 Jermyn Street
London SW1Y 6JE
00 44 (0)1451 823460
www.paxtonandwhitfield.co.uk

growers

L Booth Wild Mushroom Company, London
Wild mushrooms, fruit and vegetables.
15–16 Stoney Street
Borough Market
London SE1 9AD
00 44 (0) 20 7378 8666
Email: lboothltd@aol.com

Secretts of Milford, Surrey
Farm and farm shop.
Hurst Farm
Chapel Lane
Milford
Surrey GU8 5HU
00 44 (0)1483 520500
www.secretts.co.uk

Total Organics, London
Organic foods and salad.
Stand 21–23
Borough Market
London SE1 9AD

fish and seafood

Applebee's Fish Shop and Café, London
Fishmonger and restaurant.
5 Stoney Street
London SE1 9AA
00 44 (0)20 7407 5777
www.applebeesfish.com

Barton & Hart, London
Fishmongers.
Billingsgate Market
Trafalgar Way
London E14 5ST
00 44 (0)20 7515 2341

Loch Fyne Oysters Ltd, Argyll
Sustainable seafood suppliers.
Clachan
Cairndow
Argyll PA26 8BL
Scotland
00 44 (0)1499 600470
www.lochfyne.com

Shellseekers
Hand-dived scallops from Dartmouth, Devon and Jurassic Coast, Dorset.
Borough Market
Stoney Street
London SE1 9AD
00 44 (0)77 87516258
Email: shellseekers@talk21.com

Richard Haward's Oysters, West Mersea
Oysters.
129 Coast Road
West Mersea
Colchester
Essex CO5 8PA
00 44 (0)1206 383284
www.richardhawardsoysters.co.uk

meat

Farmer Sharp Ltd, Cumbria & Borough Market, London
Cumbrian Herdwick lamb and mutton, well-aged, Cumbrian native breed beef, naturally reared, Cumbrian pink veal and Charcuterie range.
Diamond Buildings
Pennington Lane
Lindal-in-Furness
Cumbria LA12 0LA
00 44 (0)1229 588299
www.farmersharp.co.uk

The Ginger Pig, London
Free-range farmers and butchers of rare breeds.
Borough Market
London SE1 1TL
00 44 (0)20 7403 4721
www.thegingerpig.co.uk

Johnson and Swarbrick, Lancashire
Sole producers of Goosnargh duckling and corn-fed chicken.
Swainson House Farm
Goosnargh
Preston
Lancashire PR3 2JU
00 44 (0)1772 865251
Email: johnsonandswarbrick@tiscali.co.uk

Madgett's Farm Free-range Poultry, Monmouthshire
Free-range chicken, duck, turkey and geese.
Tidenham Chase
Chepstow NP16 7LZ
00 44 (0)1291 680174
www.madgettsfarm.co.uk

M. Moen & Sons, London
High-quality butchers.
24 The Pavement
Clapham Common
London SW4 0JA
00 44 (0)20 7622 1624
www.moen.co.uk

Northfield Farm, Rutland and London
Beef, lamb, pork from Rare Breeds Trust.
Whissendine Lane
Cold Overton
Oakham
Rutland LE15 7QF
00 44 (0)16 6447 4271
www.northfieldfarm.com

Sillfield Farm, Cumbria and Borough Market, London
Rare Breeds Trust pork and wild boar, cured meats, air-dried hams and bacons, sausages, including Cumberland and gluten free. Black pudding, brawn and fresh baked pies.
Endmoor
Kendal
Cumbria LA8 0HZ
00 44 (0)15 3956 7609
www.sillfield.co.uk

beverages

**The Somerset Cider Brandy Company Ltd &
Burrow Hill Cider, Somerset**
*Somerset cider and cider brandy produced by
Julian Temperley.*
Pass Vale Farm
Burrow Hill
Kingsbury Episcopi
Martock
Somerset TA12 6BU
Tel: 00 44 (0)1460 240782
www.ciderbrandy.co.uk

Monmouth Coffee Co.
Coffee.
2 Park Street
Borough
London SE1 9AB
00 44 (0)20 7232 3010
www.monmouthcoffee.co.uk

New Forest Cider
*Traditional farmhouse cider pressed and fermented
in the New Forest.*
Littlemead
Pound Lane
Burley
Hampshire BH24 4ED
00 44 (0)14 2540 3589
www.newforestcider.co.uk

mixed produce

Brindisa Ltd, London
Spanish foods, selected and imported by Brindisa.
Floral Hall
Stoney Street
Borough Market
London SE1 9AF
00 44 (0)20 8772 1600
www.brindisa.com

Cornish Sea Salt Co., Cornwall
Pol Gwarra
Porthkerris
Lizard Peninsula
Cornwall TR12 6QJ
00 44 (0)845 337 5277
www.cornishseasalt.co.uk

Forman & Field, London
Online artisan food and drink.
Stour Road
Fish Island
London E3 2NT
00 44 (0)208 5252 352
www.formanandfield.com

Gastronomica Ltd, London
*Italian cheeses, cured meat, marinated vegetables,
pasta, wine.*
45 Tachbrook Street
London SW1V 2LZ
00 44 (0)20 7233 6656
www.gastronomica.co.uk

index

main ingredients

acknowledgements

Many thanks to Jenny Heller, Lizzy Gray and Susanna Abbott at HarperCollins whose support and guidance has been much appreciated.

Much thanks also to all the *Market Kitchen* programme production team whose work made this book possible, particularly Janice Gabriel, Michael Connock, Ashley Gorman, Jayne Hibbitt, Adam Webb, Leila Salim, Ceri Turnbull, Alan Boyle, Melanie Symonds, Anna Horsburgh, Nicole Herft, Fiona Jones and Erika John.

Further thanks to everyone else at Optomen for all their work on *Market Kitchen* and the *Market Kitchen Cookbook*, particularly Pat Llewellyn, Nicola Moody, Ben Adler, Gail Pinkerton, Helen Manley, James McGregor, Anuj Prabhu-Desai and Vanessa Land.

Thanks also to all at Good Food for their support, particularly Jane Rogerson, Jane Mote, Richard Kingsbury, Roopa Gulati, Steve Grizzell, Denise Wallin, Tamsyn Zietsman and Rebecca Schutze.

Last, but by no means least, our thanks go to Charles Walker at United Agents and to our recipe consultants, Angela Nilsen and Jeni Wright, for their testing and writing skills.